Name

_____

PICTURE

Mutation : _____

Sex : _____

Date of birth : _____ / _____ / _____

Microchip number :

Acquisition date *:*   /   /

Owner's details :

POGONA

Common Name : *Rankin's Dragon*

Family : *Agamidae*

Genus : *Pogona*

Species : *henrylawsoni*

Origin : *Australia (Queensland).*

Habitat : *Semi arid savannah, grassy plains.*

Length : *25 cm to 30 cm.*

Type *: Terrestrial.*

Temperatures :	Cooler end	Warm spot
Day	79°F (26°C)	95/104°F (35/40°C)
Night	68°F (20°C)	72°F (22°C)

Lighting : *Intense with strong UVB.*

Hygrometry : *50 %.*

HENRYLAWSONI

Vivarium – Minimum size :

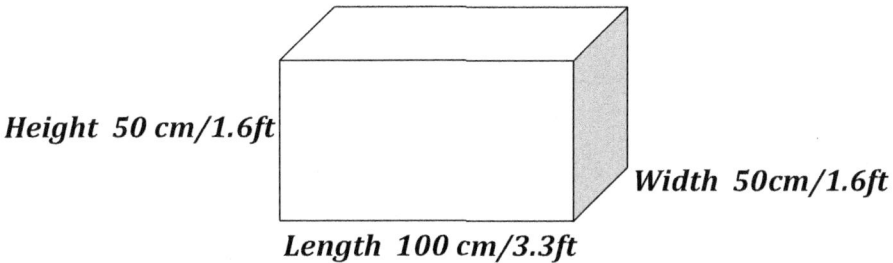

Height 50 cm/1.6ft

Width 50cm/1.6ft

Length 100 cm/3.3ft

Feeding :

 Omnivorous: reptiles, mammals, insects, spiders, veget...).ables and flowers (dandelion, clover, lamb lettuce, etc.

Reproduction :

-*Oviparous : Between 15 and 20 eggs.*
  Between 1 and 3 clutches.

-*Incubation : Between 45 and 60 days at 84°F(29°C).*

-*Sexual maturity : 2 to 3 year old.*

ADVICES — Did you know ?

✓ *Juveniles consume mostly insects. Once adult,it is imperative to mainly supply them with vegetables .*
-It is best to introduce vegetables from a young age.
-If your bearded dragon refuses vegetables, it is important to not give them insects. Be persistant !

✓ *Young mice and other mammals must begiven very rarely, other wise their life expectancy will be drastically reduced.*

✓ *Life expectancy is 15 years*

✓ *Strong UVB and calcium are mandatory.*

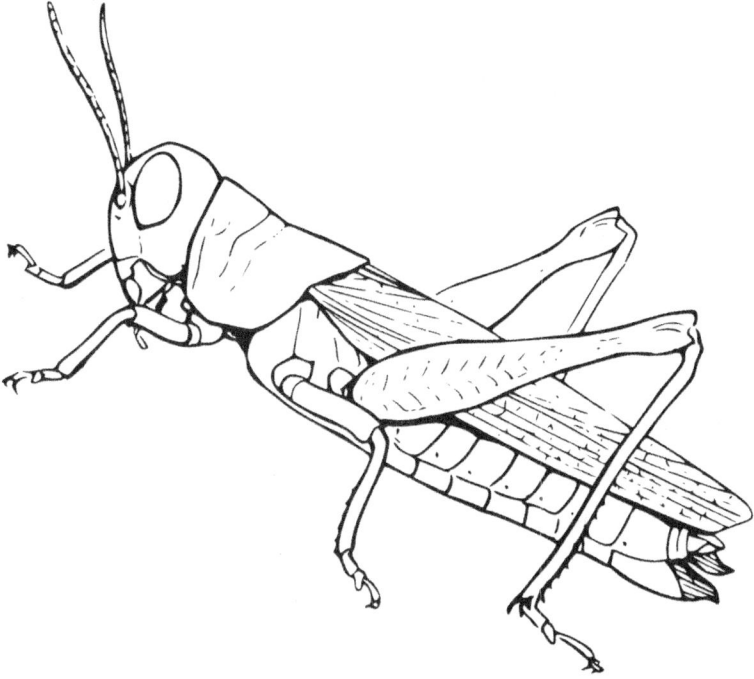

FOOD

FOOD

Date	Food Type	Comments

FOOD

Date	Food Type	Comments

FOOD

Date	Food Type	Comments

FOOD

Date	Food Type	Comments

FOOD

Date	Food Type	Comments

FOOD

Date	Food Type	Comments

FOOD

Date	Food Type	Comments

FOOD

Date	Food Type	Comments

FOOD

Date	Food Type	Comments

FOOD

Date	Food Type	Comments

FOOD

Date	Food Type	Comments

FOOD

Date	Food Type	Comments

FOOD

Date	Food Type	Comments

FOOD

Date	Food Type	Comments

FOOD

Date	Food Type	Comments

FOOD

Date	Food Type	Comments

FOOD

Date	Food Type	Comments

FOOD

Date	Food Type	Comments

FOOD

Date	Food Type	Comments

FOOD

Date	Food Type	Comments

FOOD

Date	Food Type	Comments

FOOD

Date	Food Type	Comments

FOOD

Date	Food Type	Comments

FOOD

Date	Food Type	Comments

FOOD

Date	Food Type	Comments

FOOD

Date	Food Type	Comments

FOOD

Date	Food Type	Comments

SHEDDING

SHEDDING

Date	Comments	Date	Comments

SHEDDING

Date	Comments	Date	Comments

SHEDDING

Date	Comments	Date	Comments

SHEDDING

Date	Comments	Date	Comments

SHEDDING

Date	Comments	Date	Comments

SHEDDING

Date	Comments	Date	Comments

SHEDDING

Date	Comments	Date	Comments

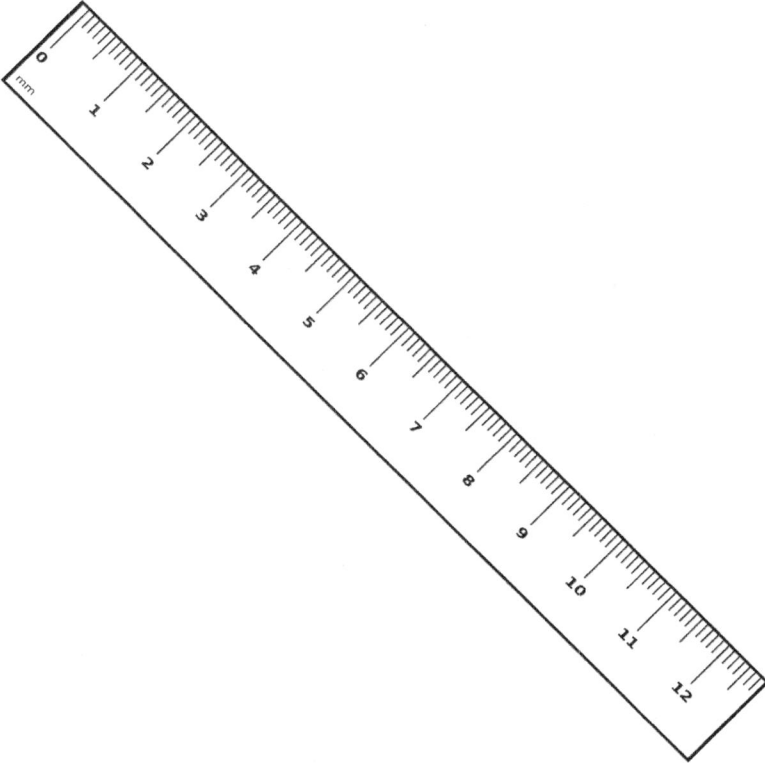

SIZE

- 12 boxes « Dates » to take a measurement every month + 2 additional boxes for intermediate readings.

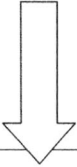

SIZE

Date	Size	Comments
03/06/2022	9cm / 4.0 ins	1
02/07/2022	13cm / 5.2 ins	2
04/08/2022	15cm / 6.0 ins	3
01/09/2022	18cm / 7.2 ins	4

- As young dragon grow quickly, the first 2 spread sheets and their graphs can be used for 6 months with a Size reading every 15 days !

- Report the dots opposite according to your corresponding statements .

GRAPH

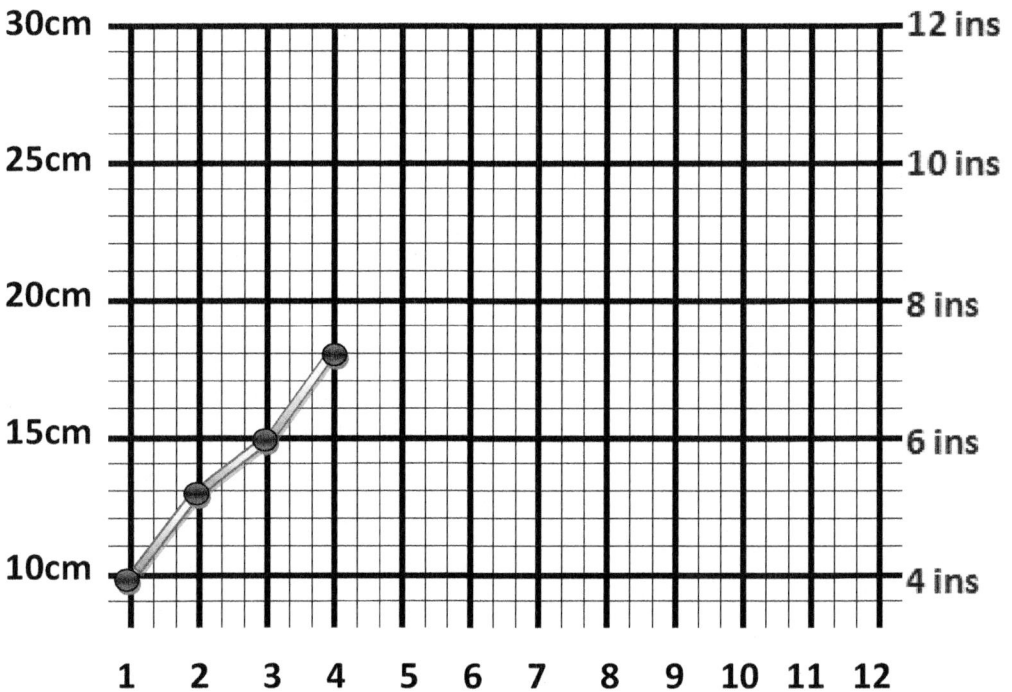

- Connect the dots and make your own graph !

SIZE (1)

Date	Size	Comments

GRAPH

40cm												16 ins

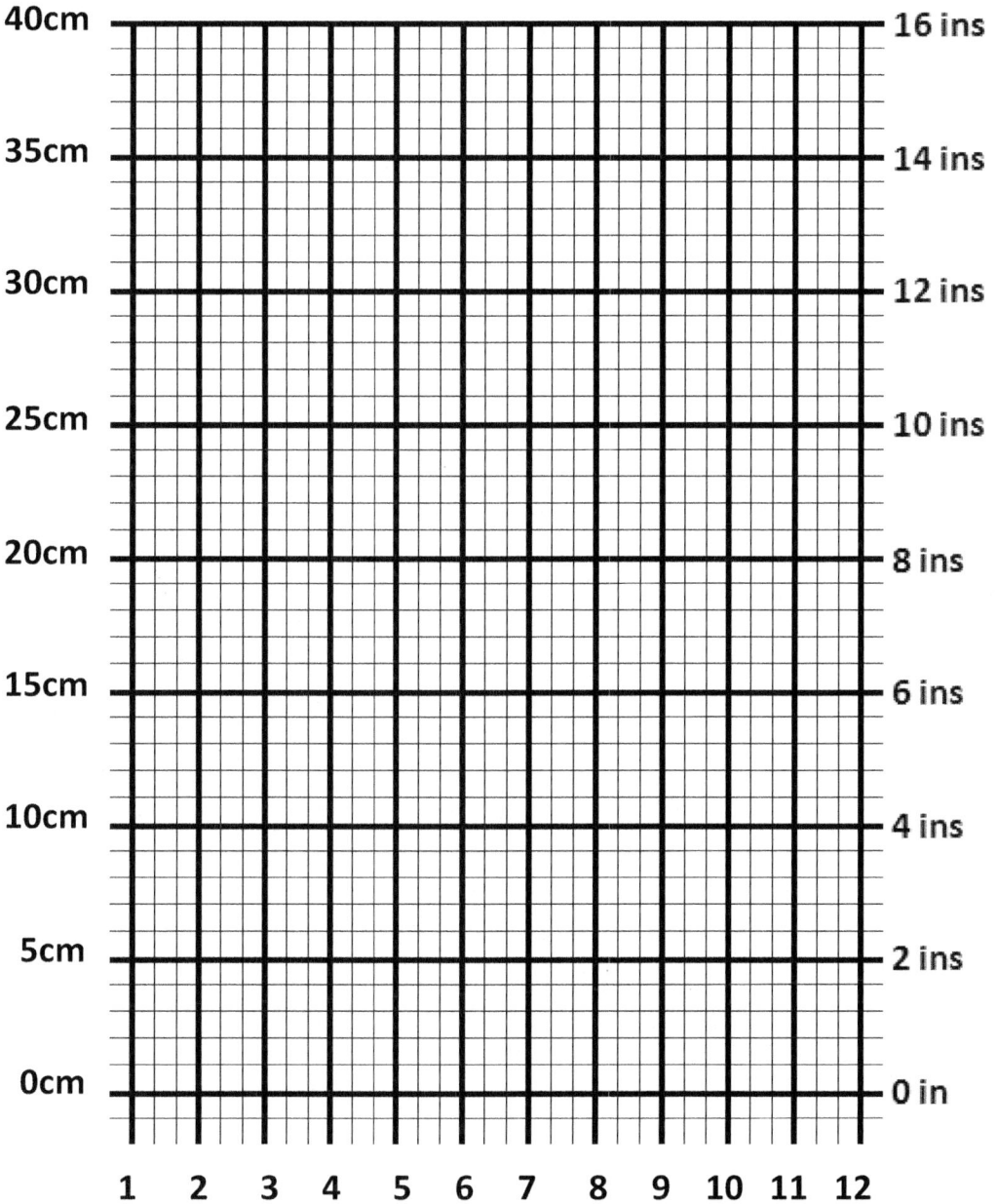

40cm	16 ins
35cm	14 ins
30cm	12 ins
25cm	10 ins
20cm	8 ins
15cm	6 ins
10cm	4 ins
5cm	2 ins
0cm	0 in

1 2 3 4 5 6 7 8 9 10 11 12

47

SIZE (2)

Date	Size	Comments

GRAPH

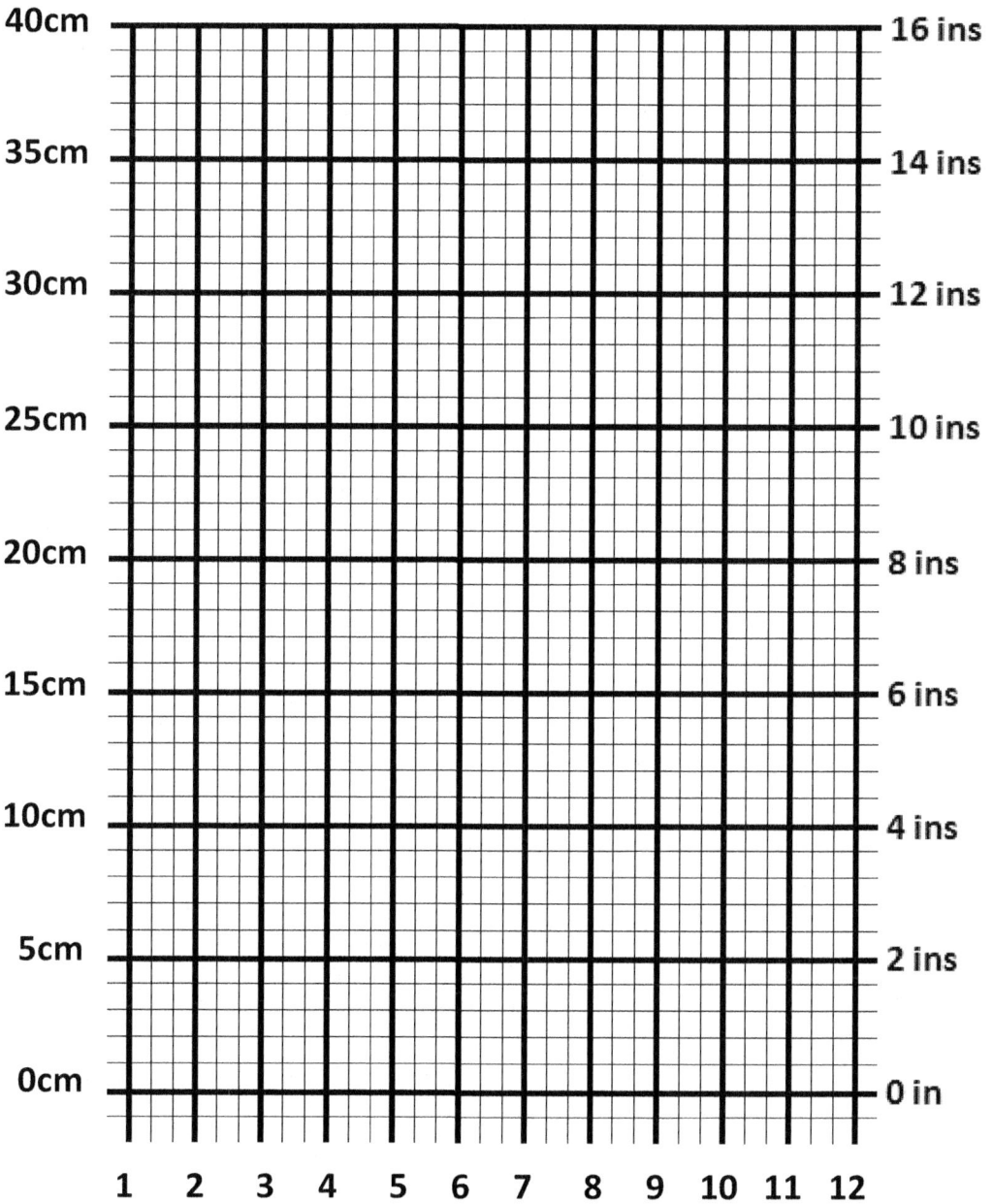

40cm — 16 ins
35cm — 14 ins
30cm — 12 ins
25cm — 10 ins
20cm — 8 ins
15cm — 6 ins
10cm — 4 ins
5cm — 2 ins
0cm — 0 in

1 2 3 4 5 6 7 8 9 10 11 12

49

SIZE (3)

Date	Size	Comments

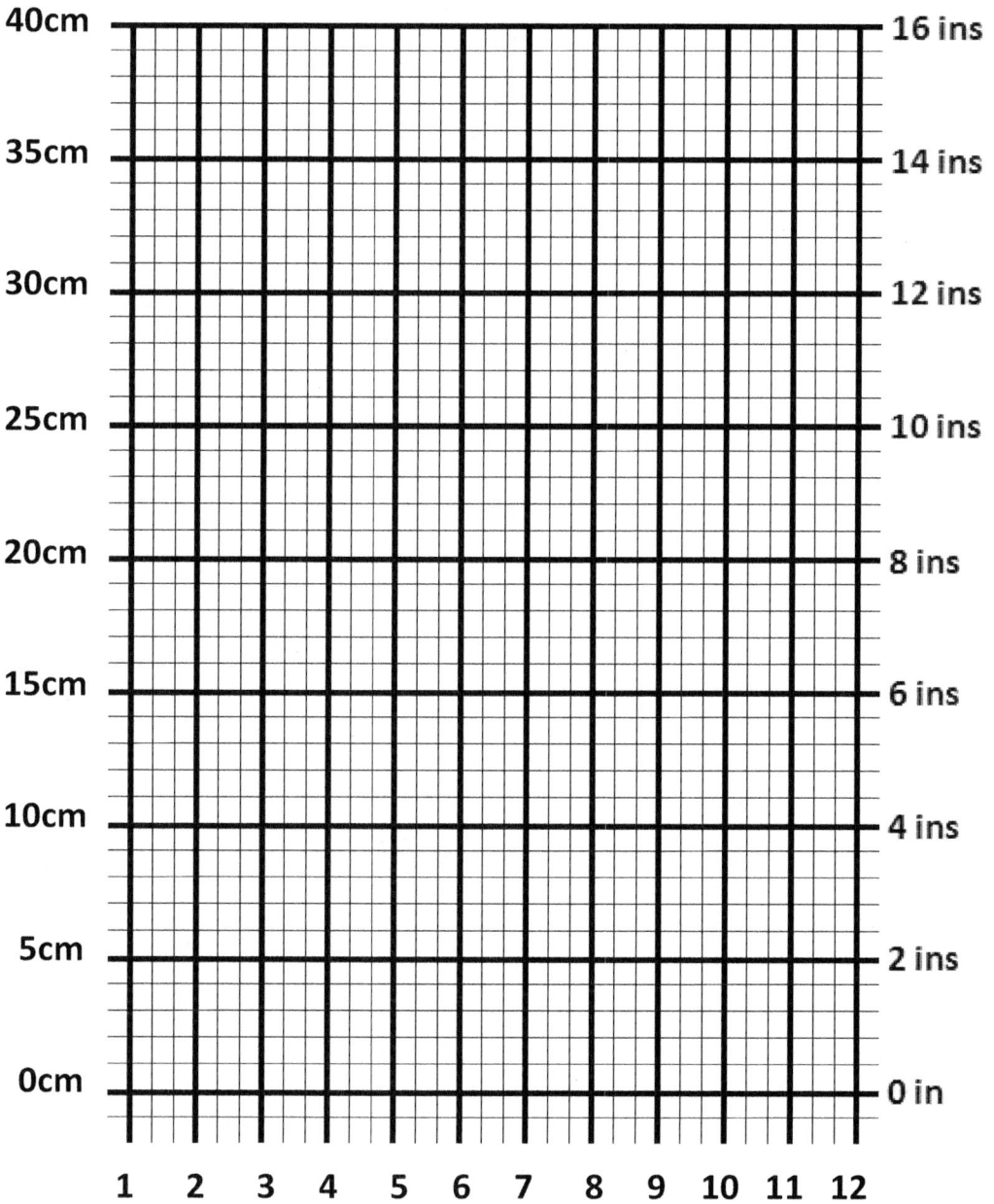

GRAPH

40cm												16 ins
35cm												14 ins
30cm												12 ins
25cm												10 ins
20cm												8 ins
15cm												6 ins
10cm												4 ins
5cm												2 ins
0cm												0 in

1   2   3   4   5   6   7   8   9   10   11   12

SIZE (4)

Date	Size	Comments

GRAPH

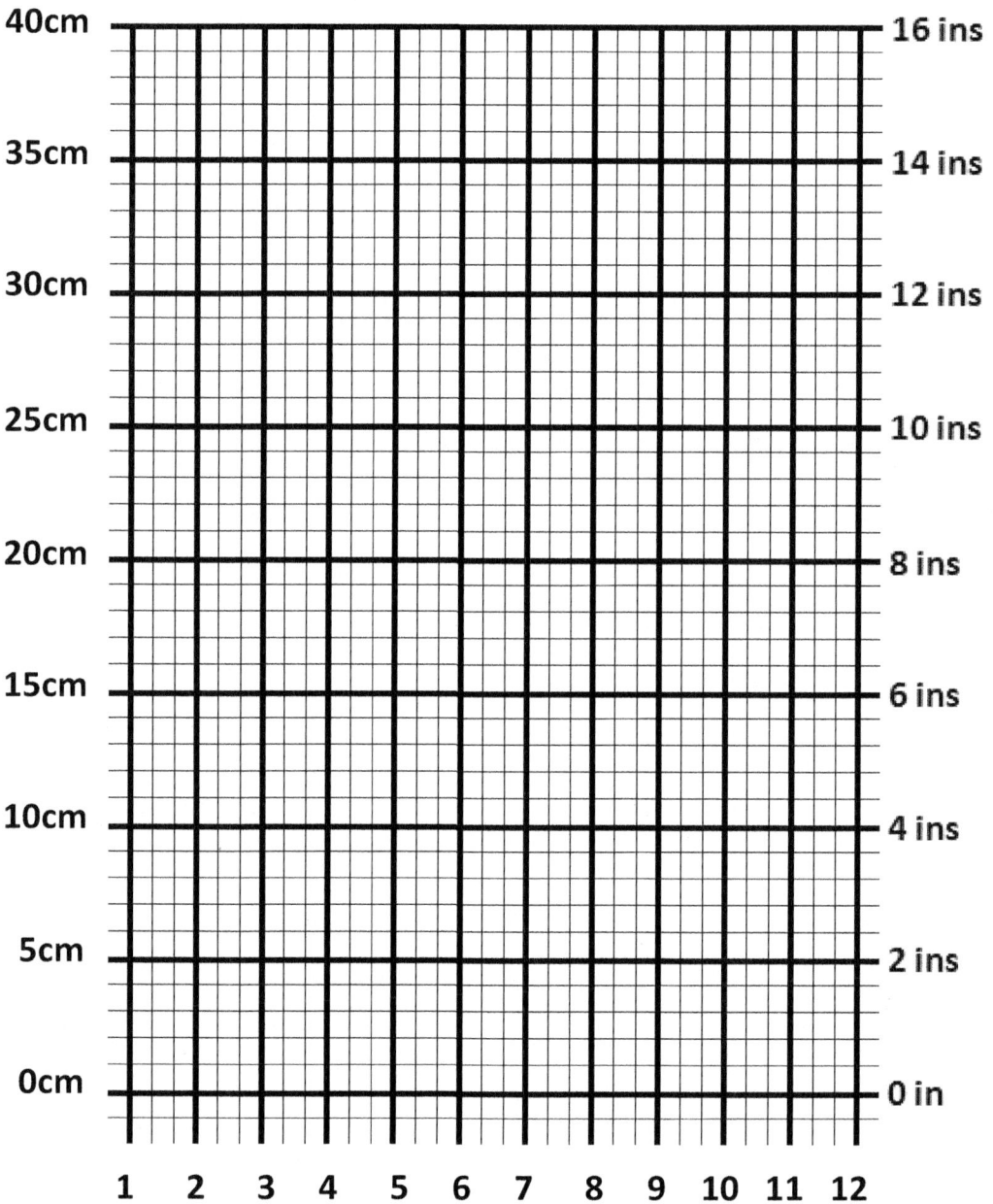

SIZE (5)

Date	Size	Comments

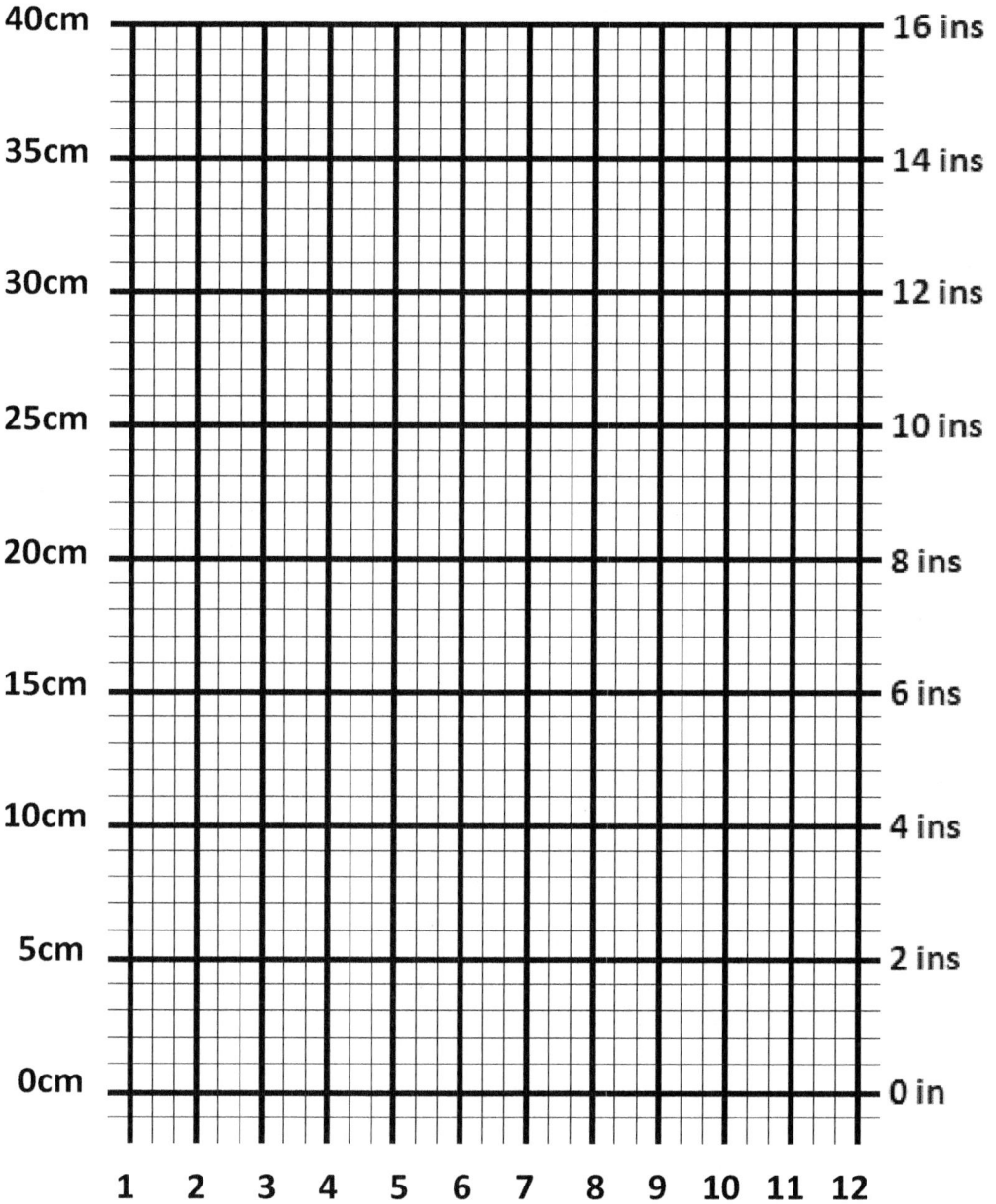

GRAPH

40cm													16 ins
35cm													14 ins
30cm													12 ins
25cm													10 ins
20cm													8 ins
15cm													6 ins
10cm													4 ins
5cm													2 ins
0cm													0 in

1 2 3 4 5 6 7 8 9 10 11 12

SIZE (6)

Date	Size	Comments

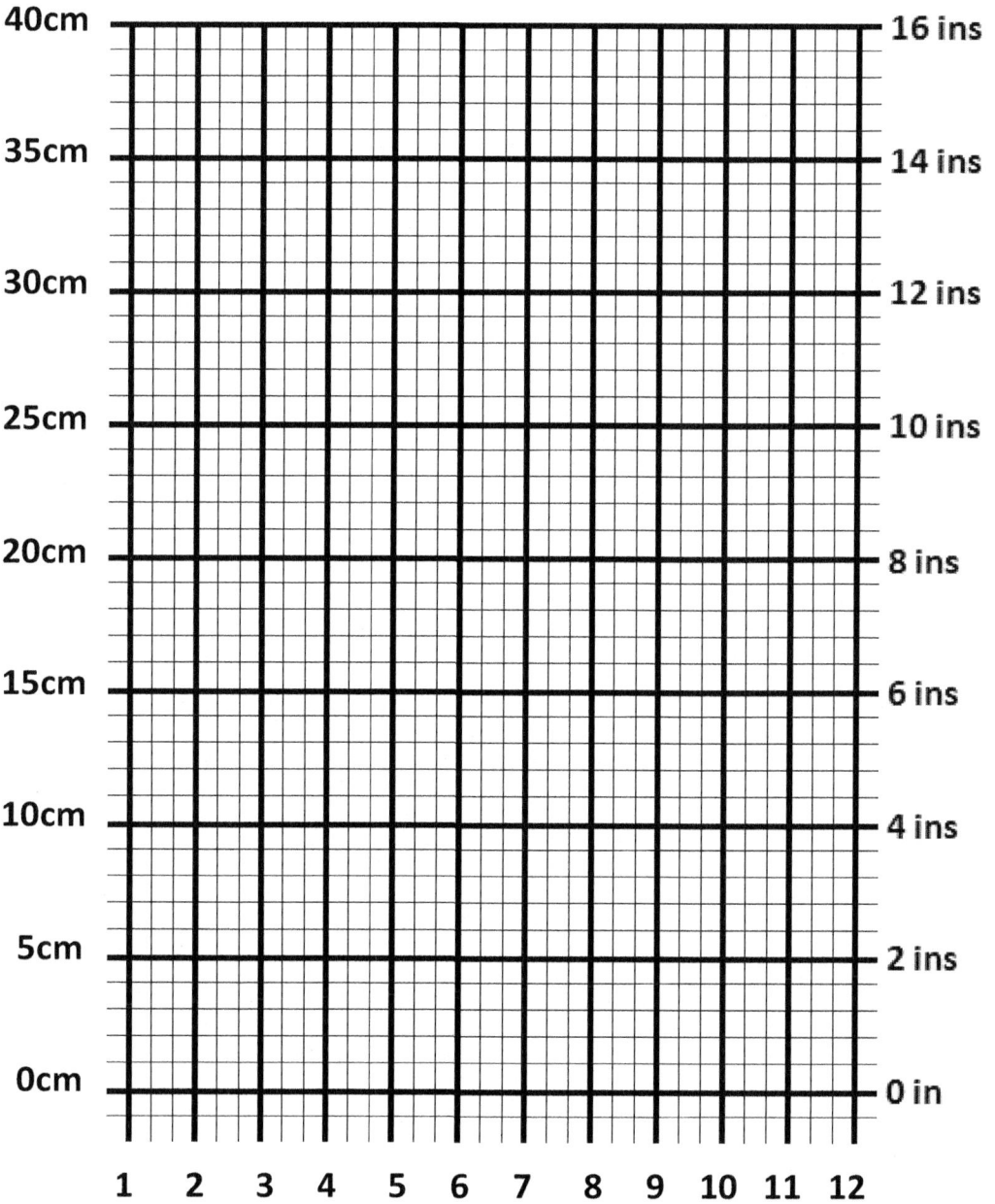

GRAPH

40cm												16 ins
35cm												14 ins
30cm												12 ins
25cm												10 ins
20cm												8 ins
15cm												6 ins
10cm												4 ins
5cm												2 ins
0cm												0 in

1 2 3 4 5 6 7 8 9 10 11 12

SIZE (7)

Date	Size	Comments

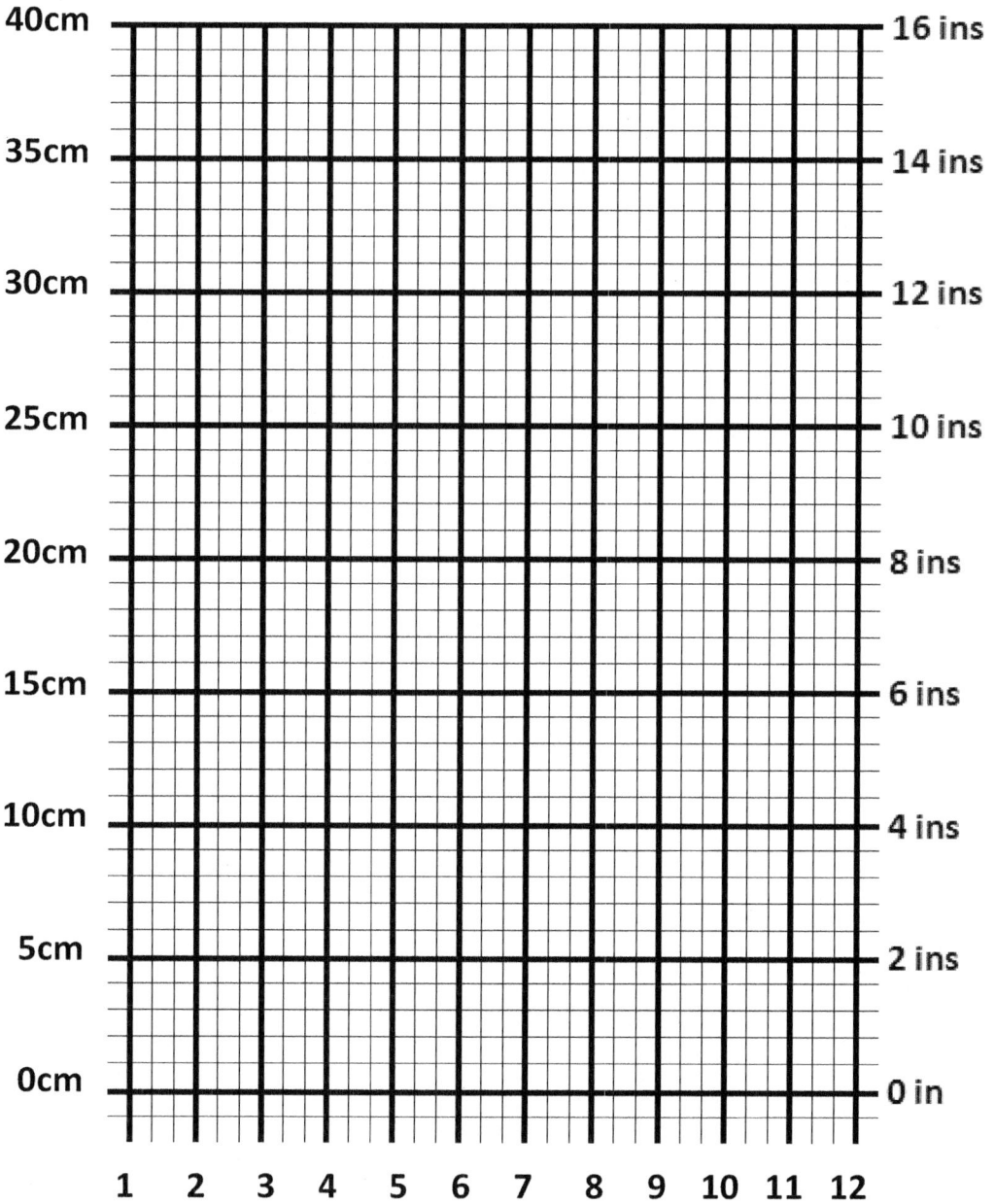

GRAPH

40cm												16 ins
35cm												14 ins
30cm												12 ins
25cm												10 ins
20cm												8 ins
15cm												6 ins
10cm												4 ins
5cm												2 ins
0cm												0 in

1   2   3   4   5   6   7   8   9   10   11   12

SIZE (8)

Date	Size	Comments

GRAPH

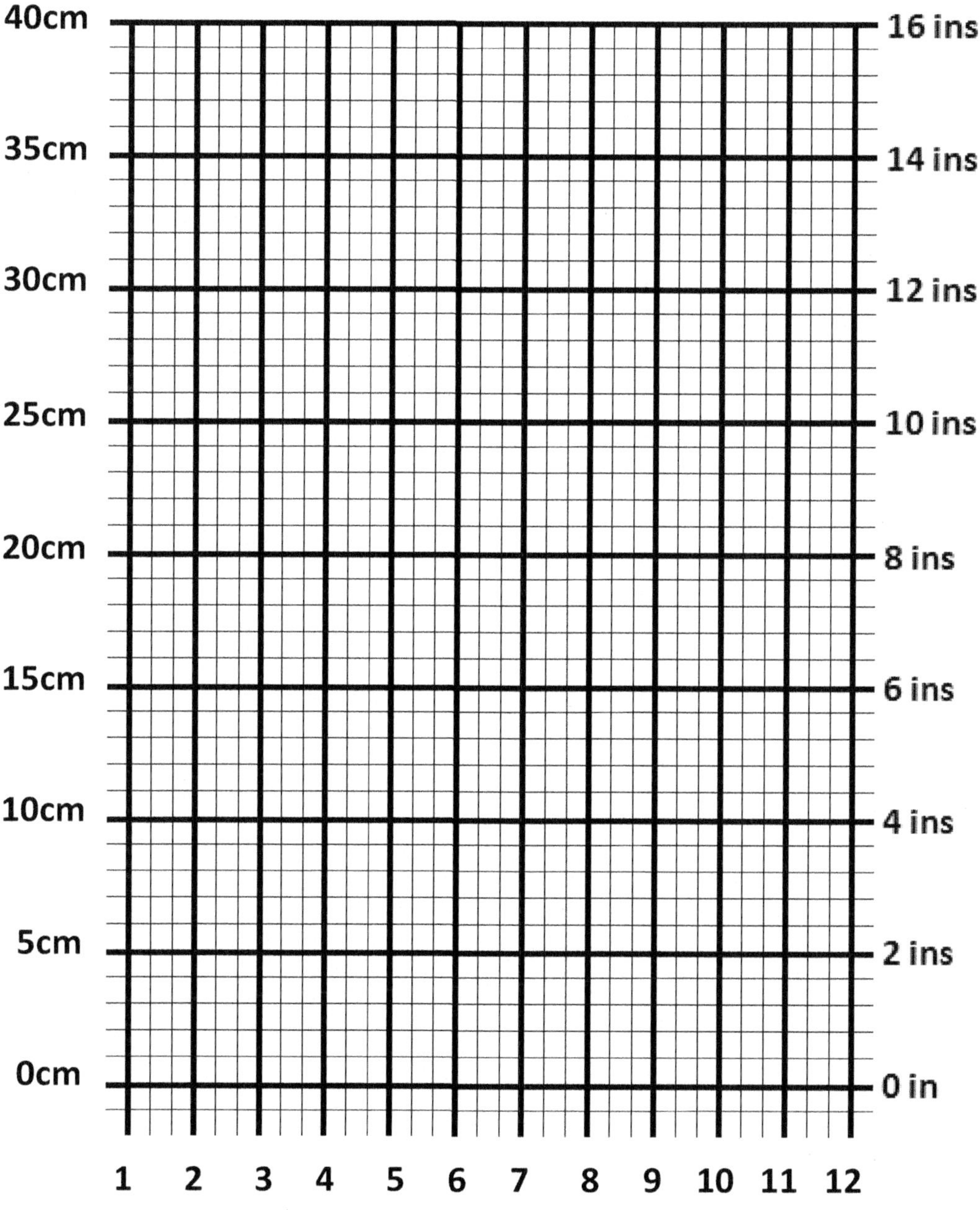
40cm
35cm
30cm
25cm
20cm
15cm
10cm
5cm
0cm
16 ins
14 ins
12 ins
10 ins
8 ins
6 ins
4 ins
2 ins
0 in
1
2
3
4
5
6
7
8
9
10
11
12

SIZE (9)

Date	Size	Comments

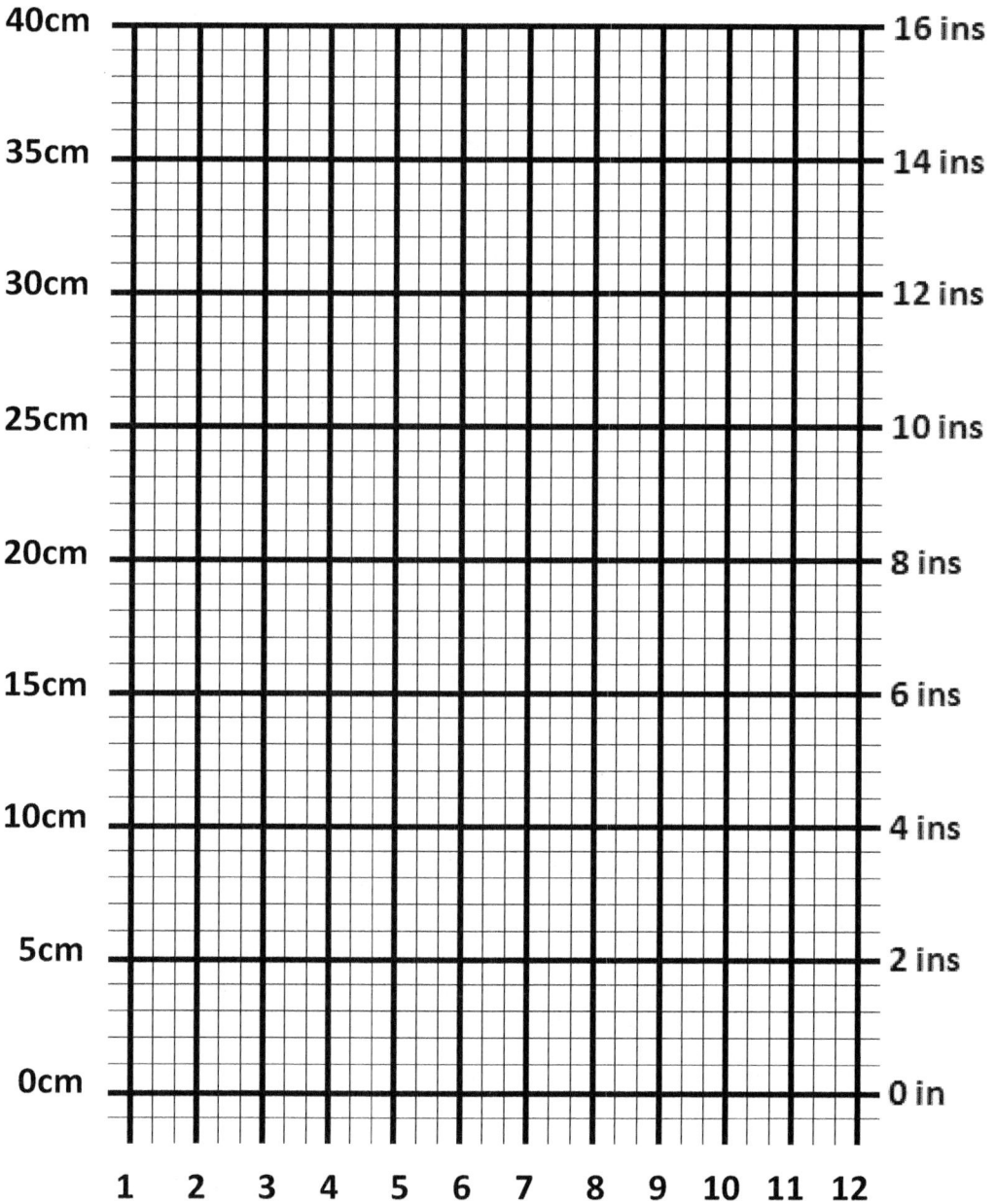

GRAPH

40cm													16 ins
35cm													14 ins
30cm													12 ins
25cm													10 ins
20cm													8 ins
15cm													6 ins
10cm													4 ins
5cm													2 ins
0cm													0 in

1   2   3   4   5   6   7   8   9   10   11   12

SIZE (10)

Date	Size	Comments

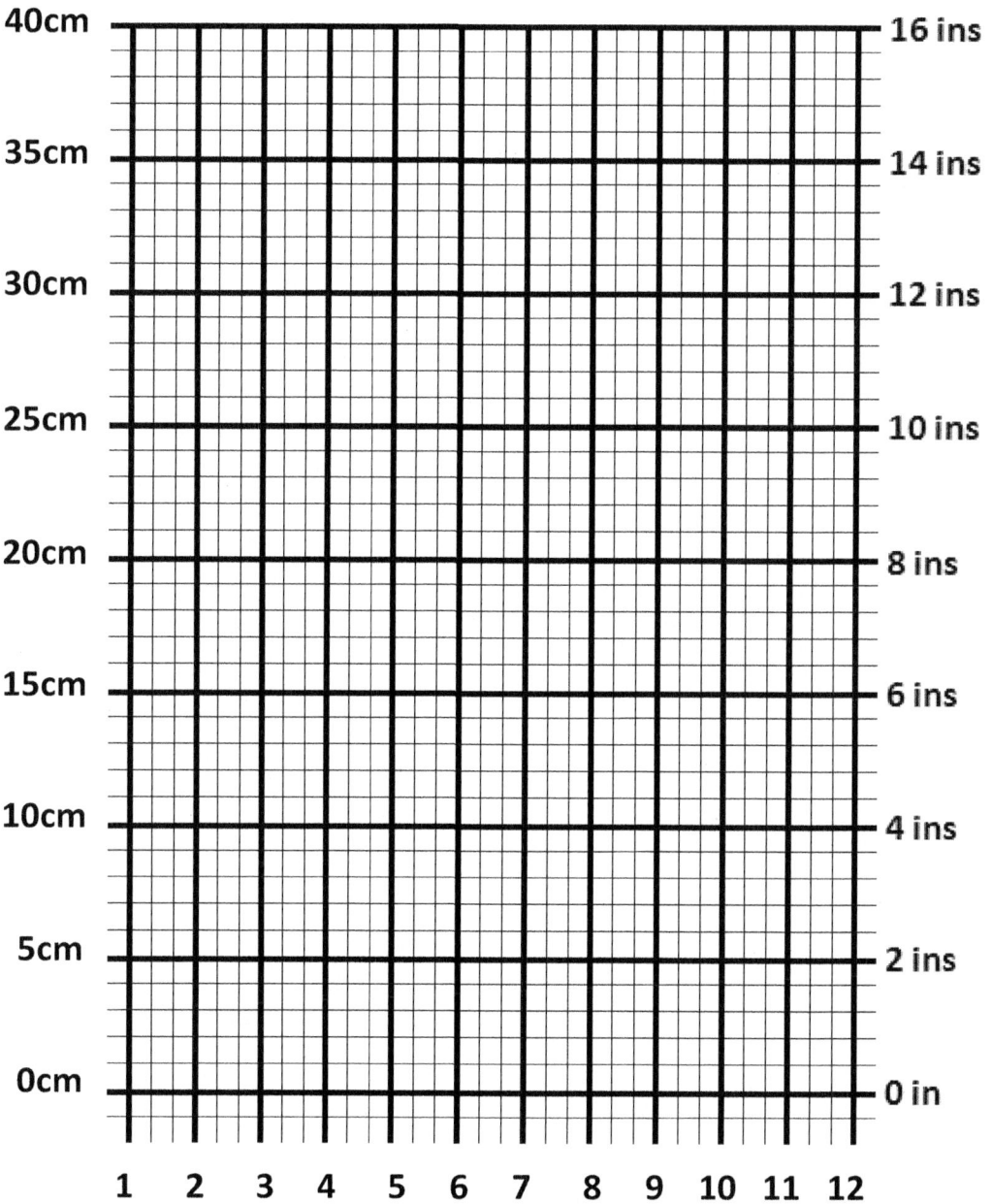

GRAPH

40cm												16 ins
35cm												14 ins
30cm												12 ins
25cm												10 ins
20cm												8 ins
15cm												6 ins
10cm												4 ins
5cm												2 ins
0cm												0 in

1 2 3 4 5 6 7 8 9 10 11 12

SIZE (11)

Date	Size	Comments

GRAPH

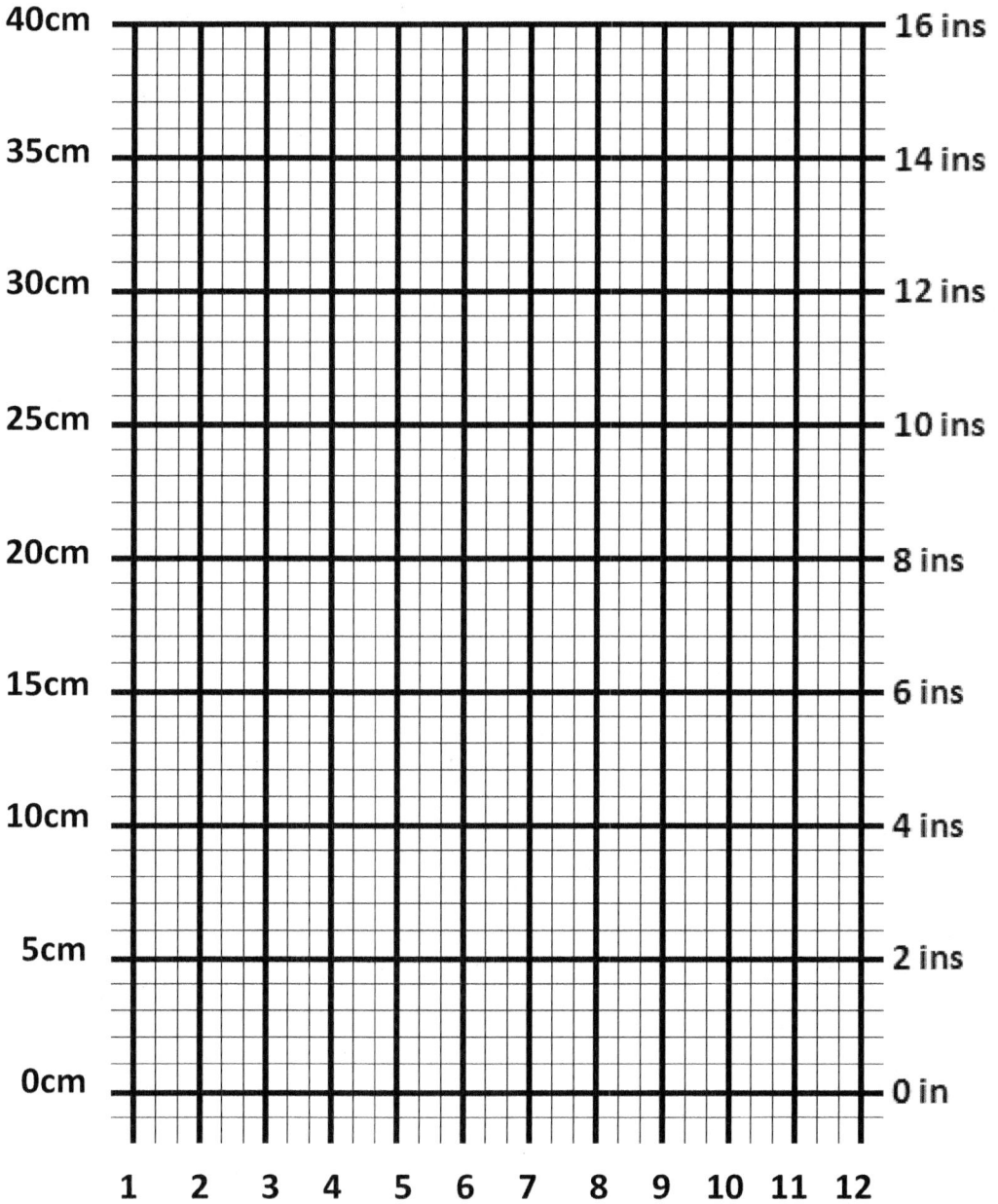

SIZE (12)

Date	Size	Comments

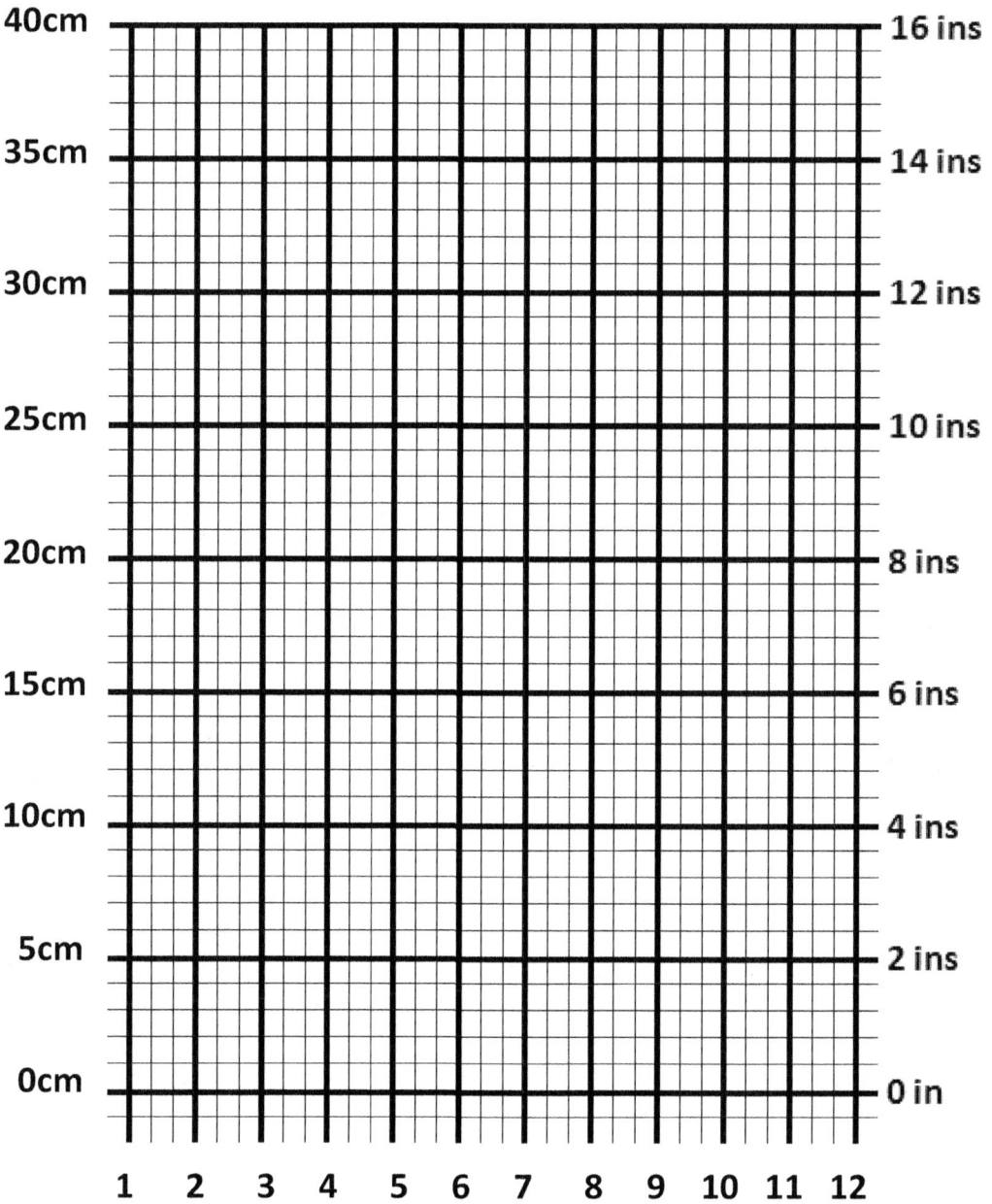

GRAPH

40cm	16 ins
35cm	14 ins
30cm	12 ins
25cm	10 ins
20cm	8 ins
15cm	6 ins
10cm	4 ins
5cm	2 ins
0cm	0 in

1   2   3   4   5   6   7   8   9   10   11   12

<u>COMMENTS</u>

WEIGHT

- 12 boxes « dates » to take a measurement every month + 2 additional boxes for intermediate readings.

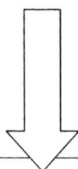

WEIGHT

Date	Weight		Comments
03/06/2022	48g / 2.0oz	1	
02/07/2022	80g / 3.2oz	2	
04/08/2022	100g / 4.0oz	3	
01/09/2022	130g / 5.2oz	4	

- As young dragon grow quickly, the first 2 spread sheets and their graphs can be used for 6 months with a weight reading every 15 days.

- Report the dots opposite according to your corresponding statements.

GRAPH

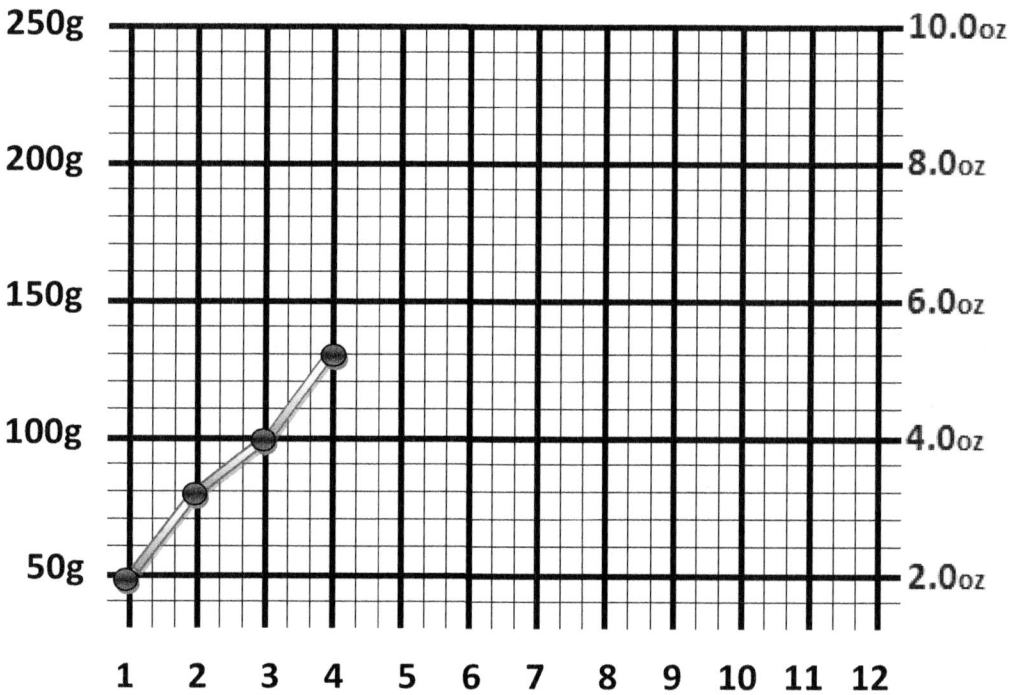

- Connect the dots and make your own graph.

WEIGHT (1)

Date	Weight	Comments

GRAPH

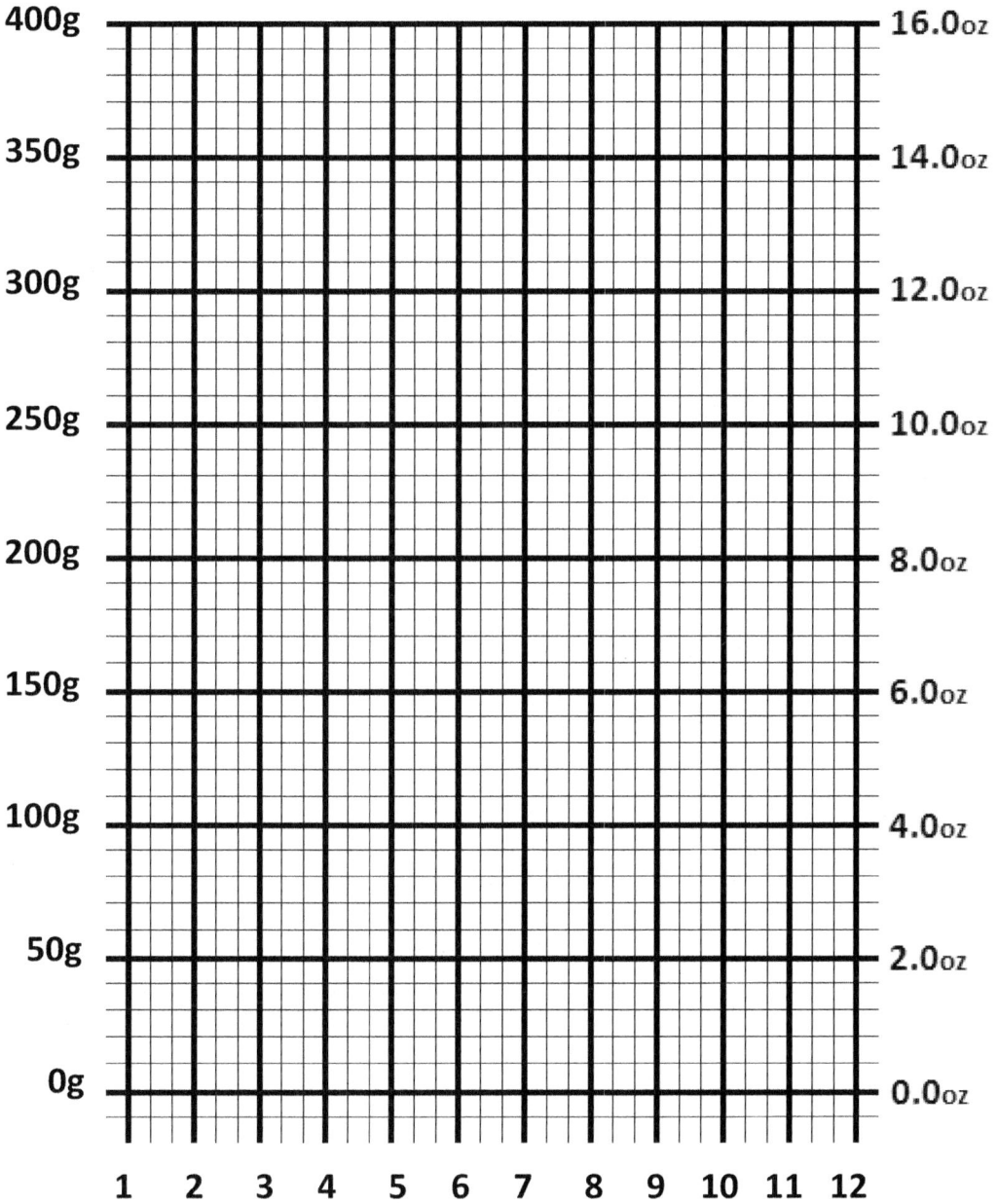

WEIGHT (2)

Date	Weight	Comments

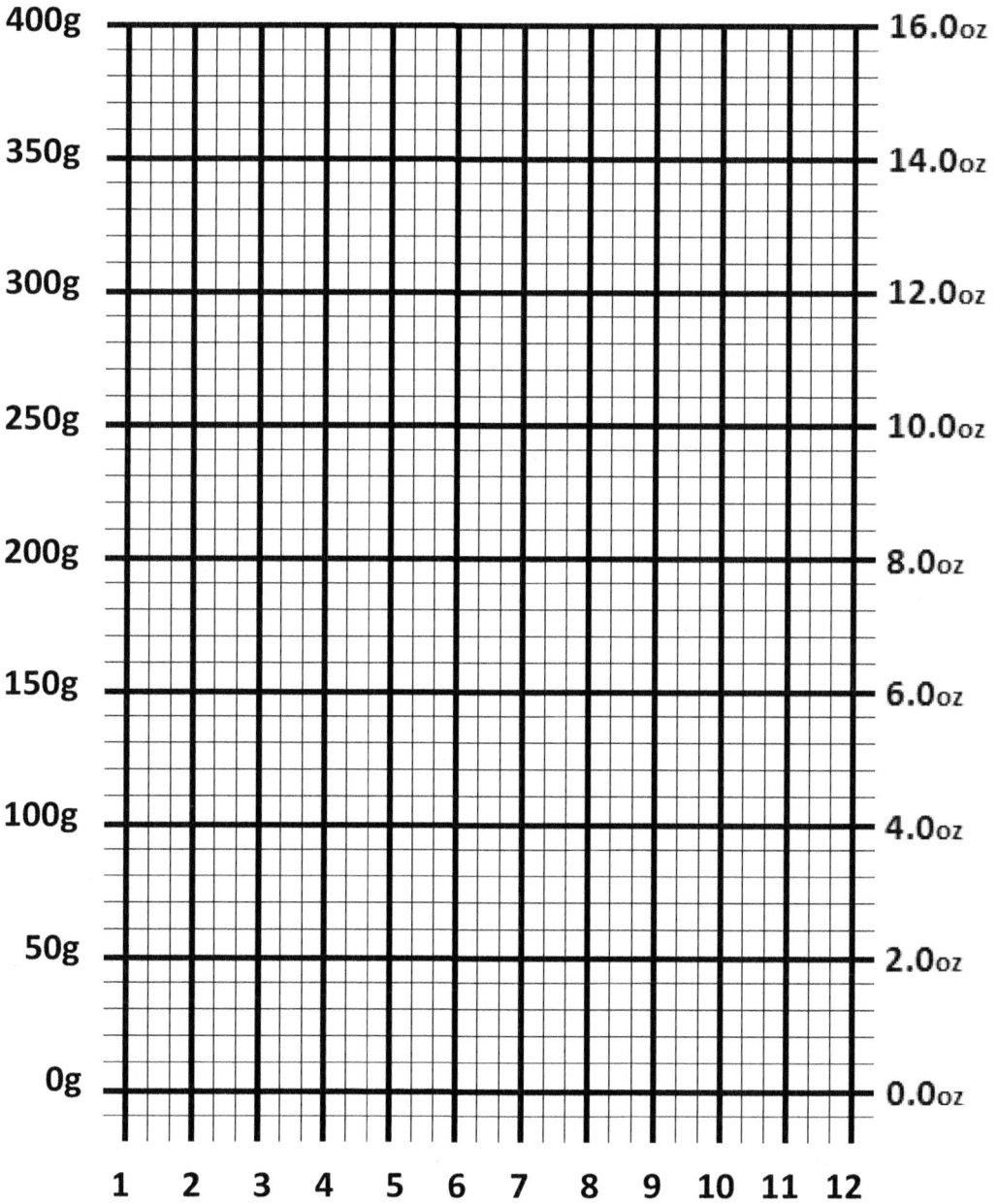

GRAPH

400g		16.0oz
350g		14.0oz
300g		12.0oz
250g		10.0oz
200g		8.0oz
150g		6.0oz
100g		4.0oz
50g		2.0oz
0g		0.0oz

1 2 3 4 5 6 7 8 9 10 11 12

WEIGHT (3)

Date	Weight	Comments

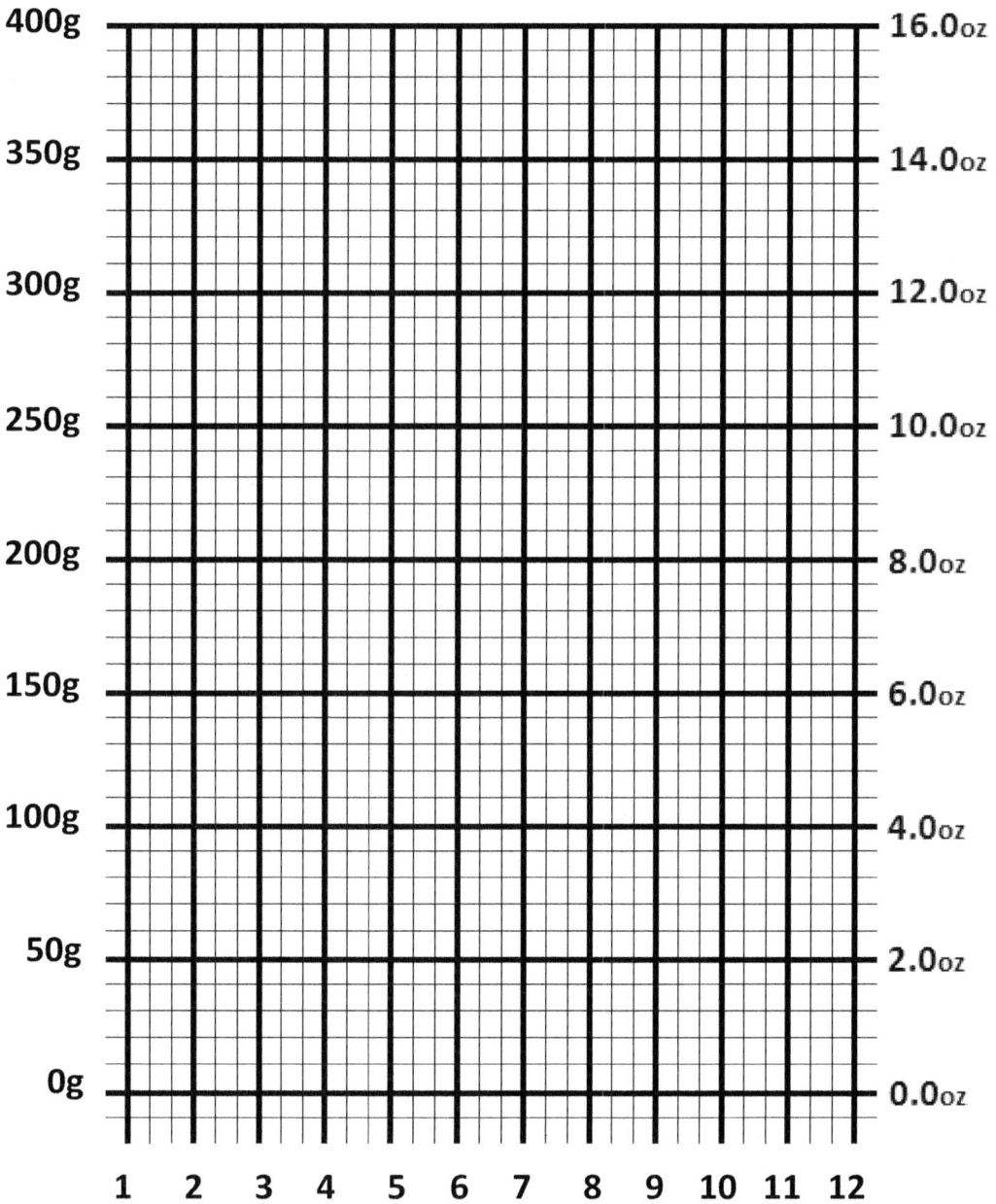

GRAPH

400g													16.0oz
350g													14.0oz
300g													12.0oz
250g													10.0oz
200g													8.0oz
150g													6.0oz
100g													4.0oz
50g													2.0oz
0g													0.0oz

1 2 3 4 5 6 7 8 9 10 11 12

WEIGHT (4)

Date	Weight	Comments

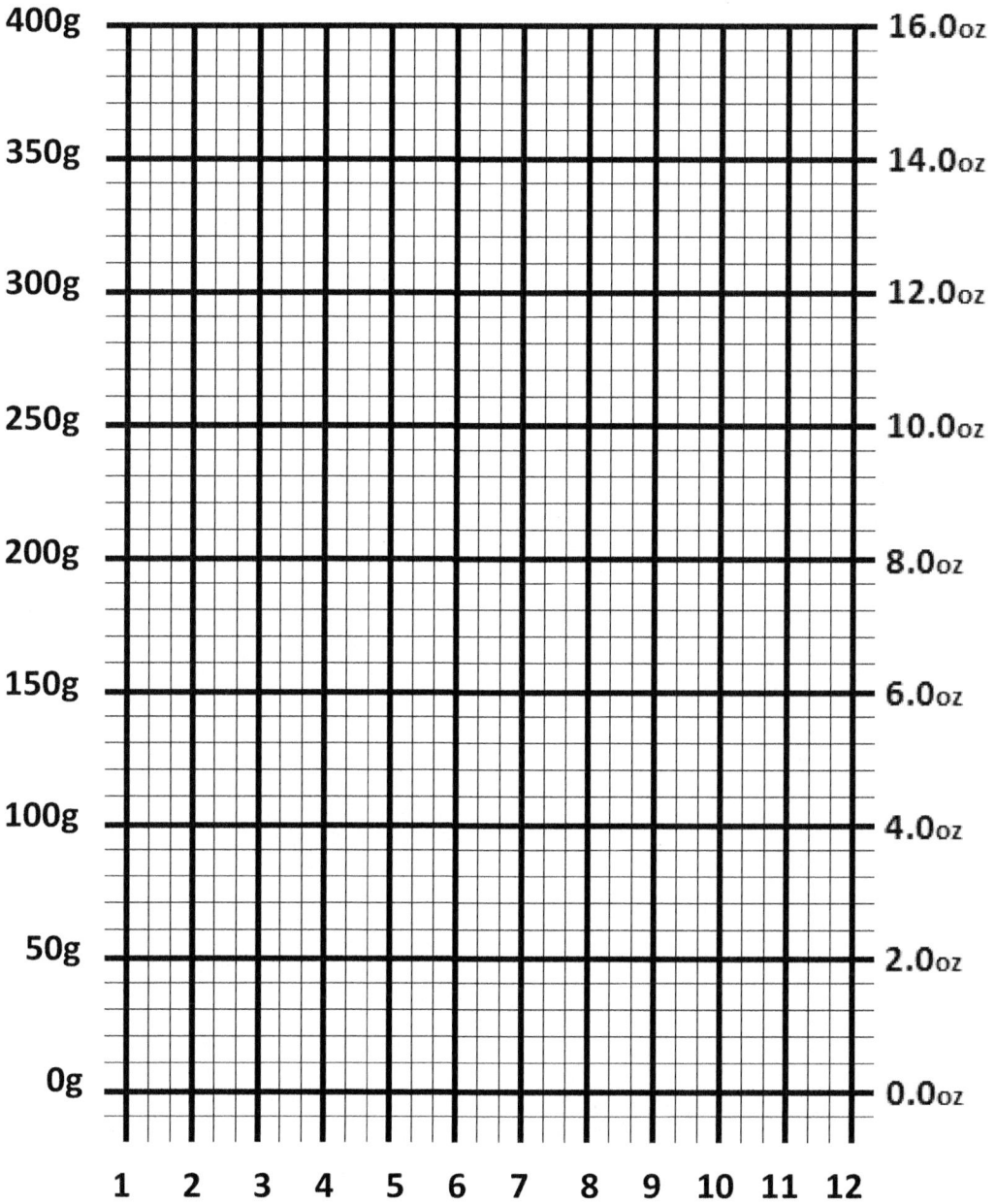

GRAPH

400g												16.0oz
350g												14.0oz
300g												12.0oz
250g												10.0oz
200g												8.0oz
150g												6.0oz
100g												4.0oz
50g												2.0oz
0g												0.0oz

1   2   3   4   5   6   7   8   9   10   11   12

WEIGHT (5)

Date	Weight	Comments

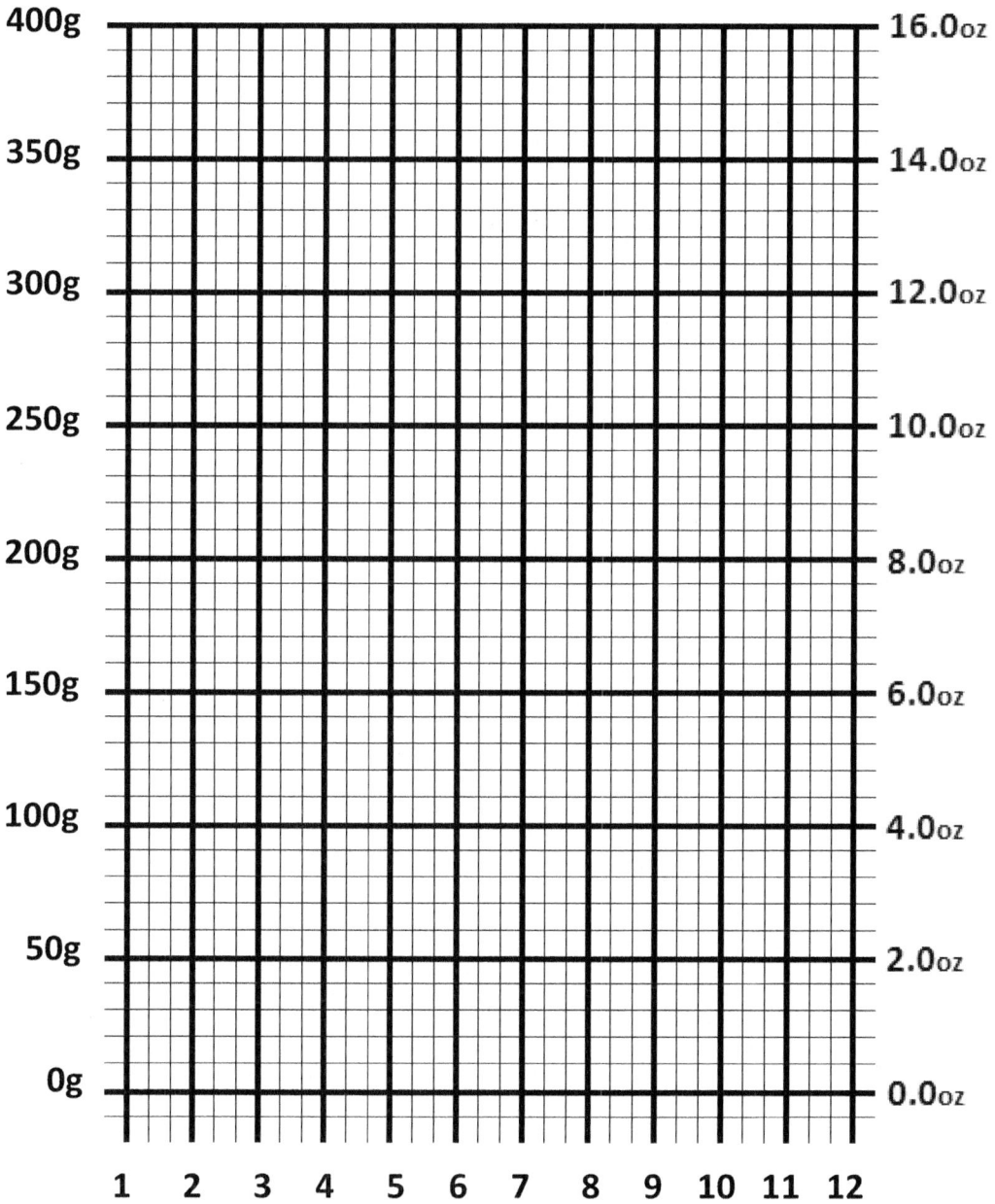

GRAPH

	1	2	3	4	5	6	7	8	9	10	11	12	
400g													16.0oz
350g													14.0oz
300g													12.0oz
250g													10.0oz
200g													8.0oz
150g													6.0oz
100g													4.0oz
50g													2.0oz
0g													0.0oz

WEIGHT (6)

Date	Weight	Comments

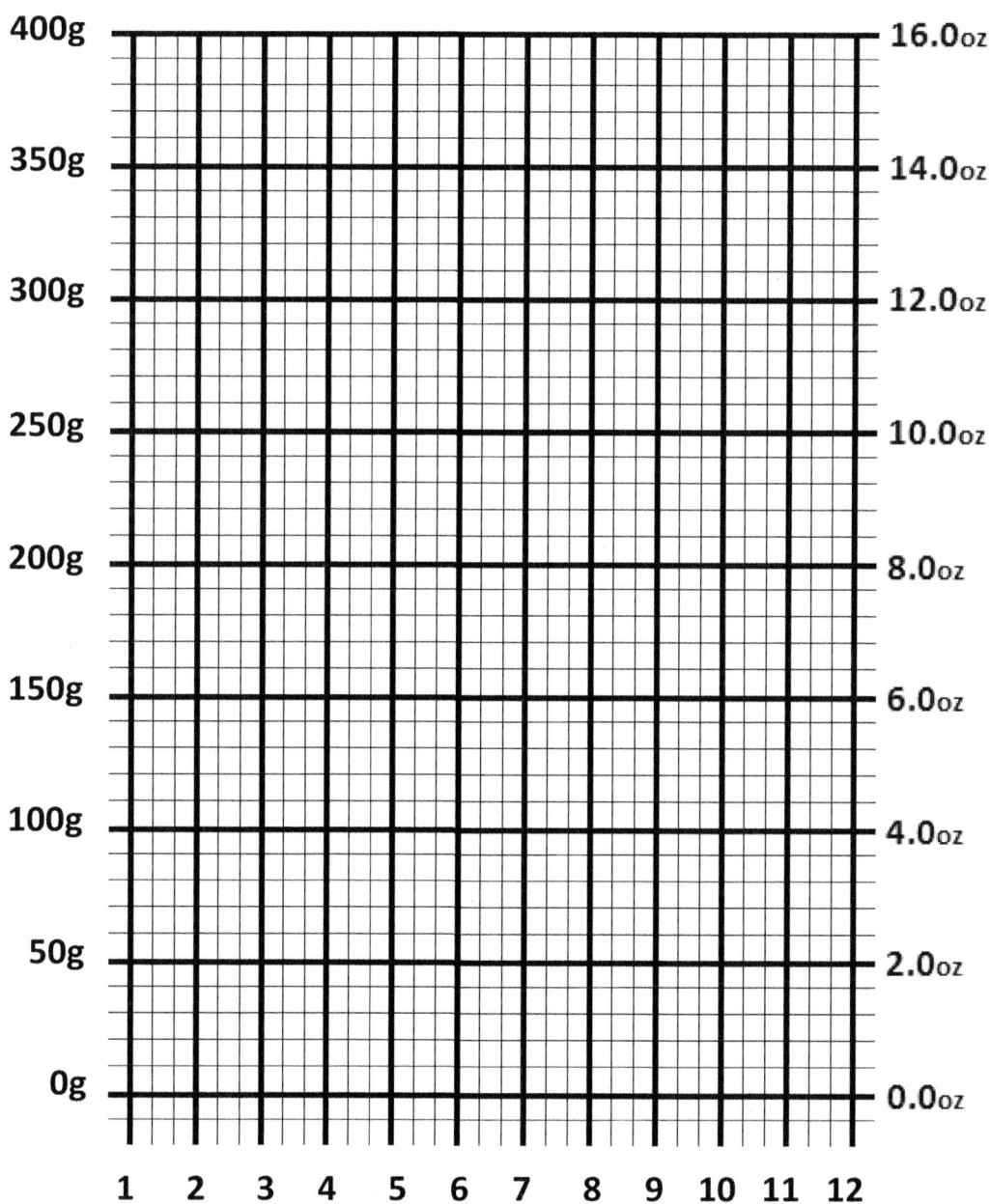

GRAPH

	400g												16.0oz
	350g												14.0oz
	300g												12.0oz
	250g												10.0oz
	200g												8.0oz
	150g												6.0oz
	100g												4.0oz
	50g												2.0oz
	0g												0.0oz

1   2   3   4   5   6   7   8   9   10   11   12

WEIGHT (7)

Date	Weight	Comments

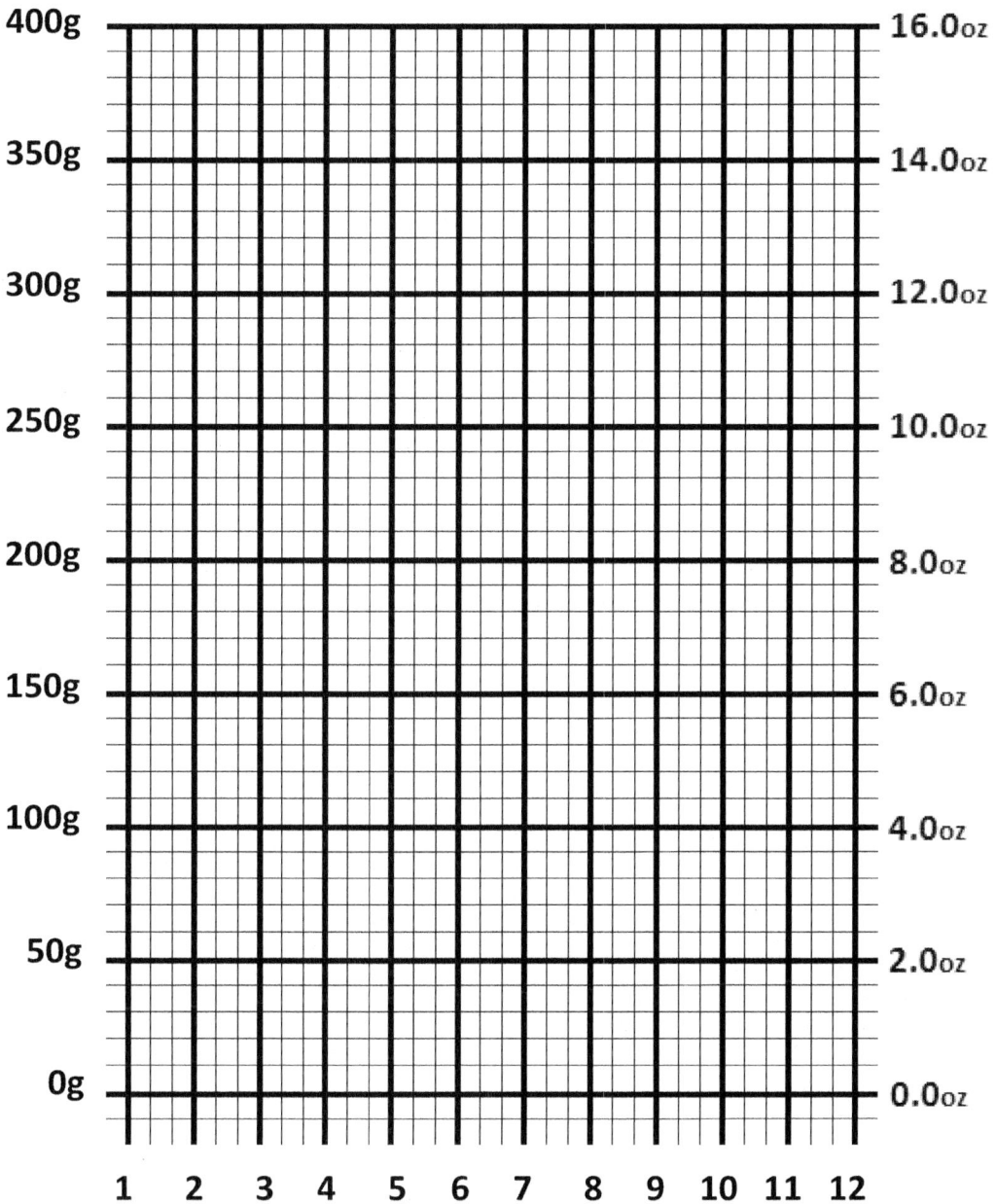

GRAPH

400g — ... — 16.0oz

350g — ... — 14.0oz

300g — ... — 12.0oz

250g — ... — 10.0oz

200g — ... — 8.0oz

150g — ... — 6.0oz

100g — ... — 4.0oz

50g — ... — 2.0oz

0g — ... — 0.0oz

1   2   3   4   5   6   7   8   9   10   11   12

WEIGHT (8)

Date	Weight	Comments

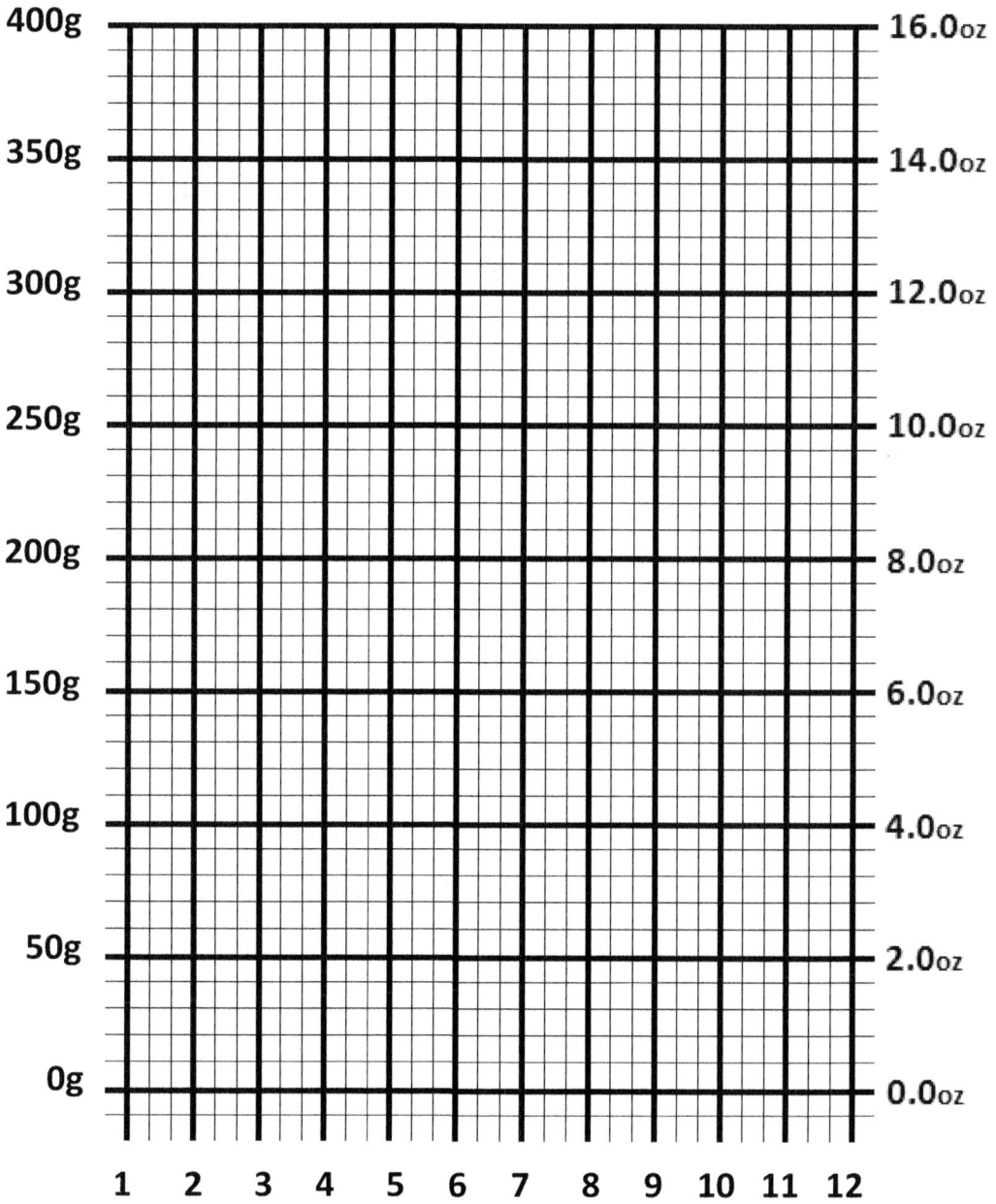

GRAPH

400g			16.0oz
350g			14.0oz
300g			12.0oz
250g			10.0oz
200g			8.0oz
150g			6.0oz
100g			4.0oz
50g			2.0oz
0g			0.0oz

1   2   3   4   5   6   7   8   9   10   11   12

WEIGHT (9)

Date	Weight	Comments

GRAPH

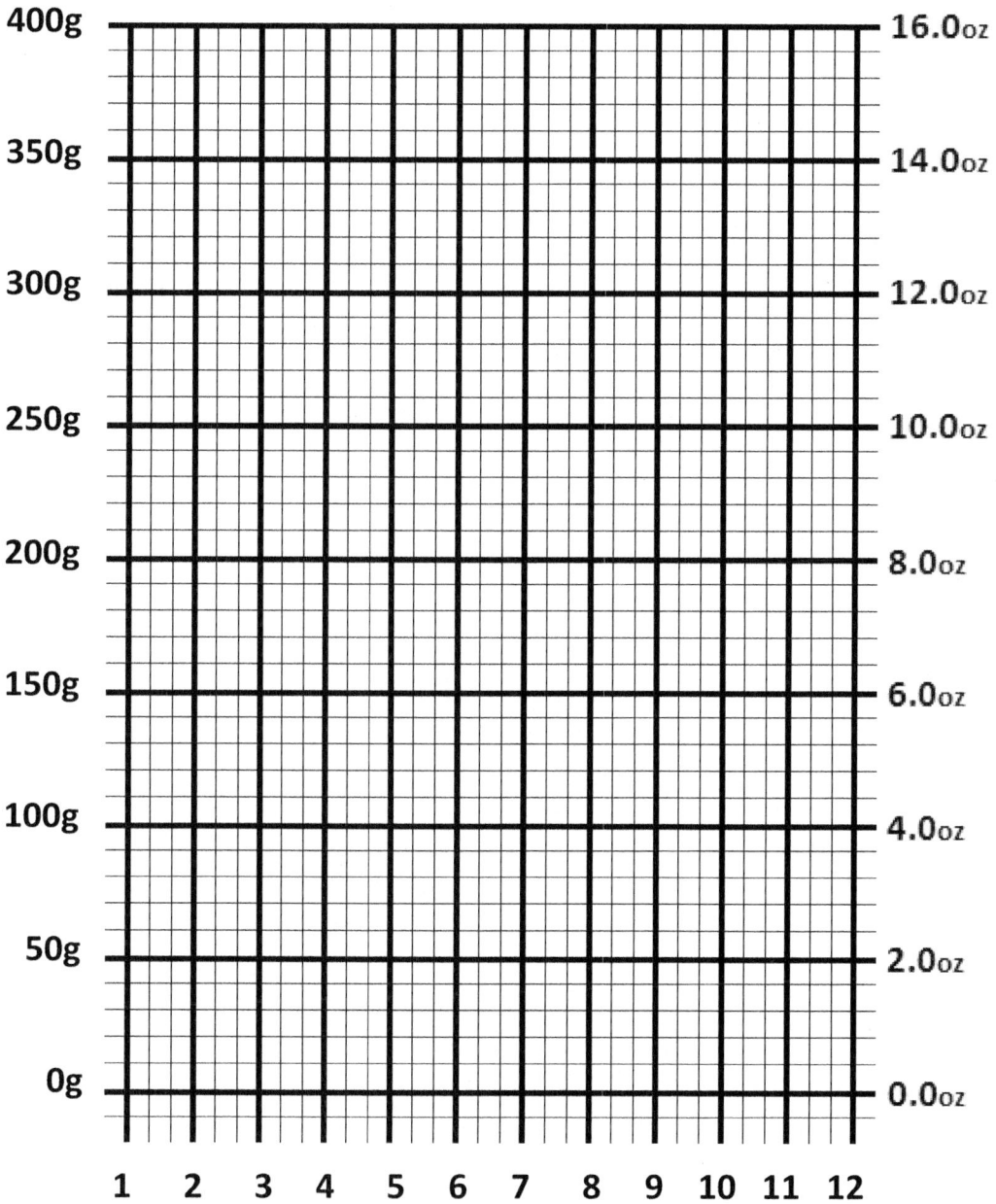

WEIGHT (10)

Date	Weight	Comments

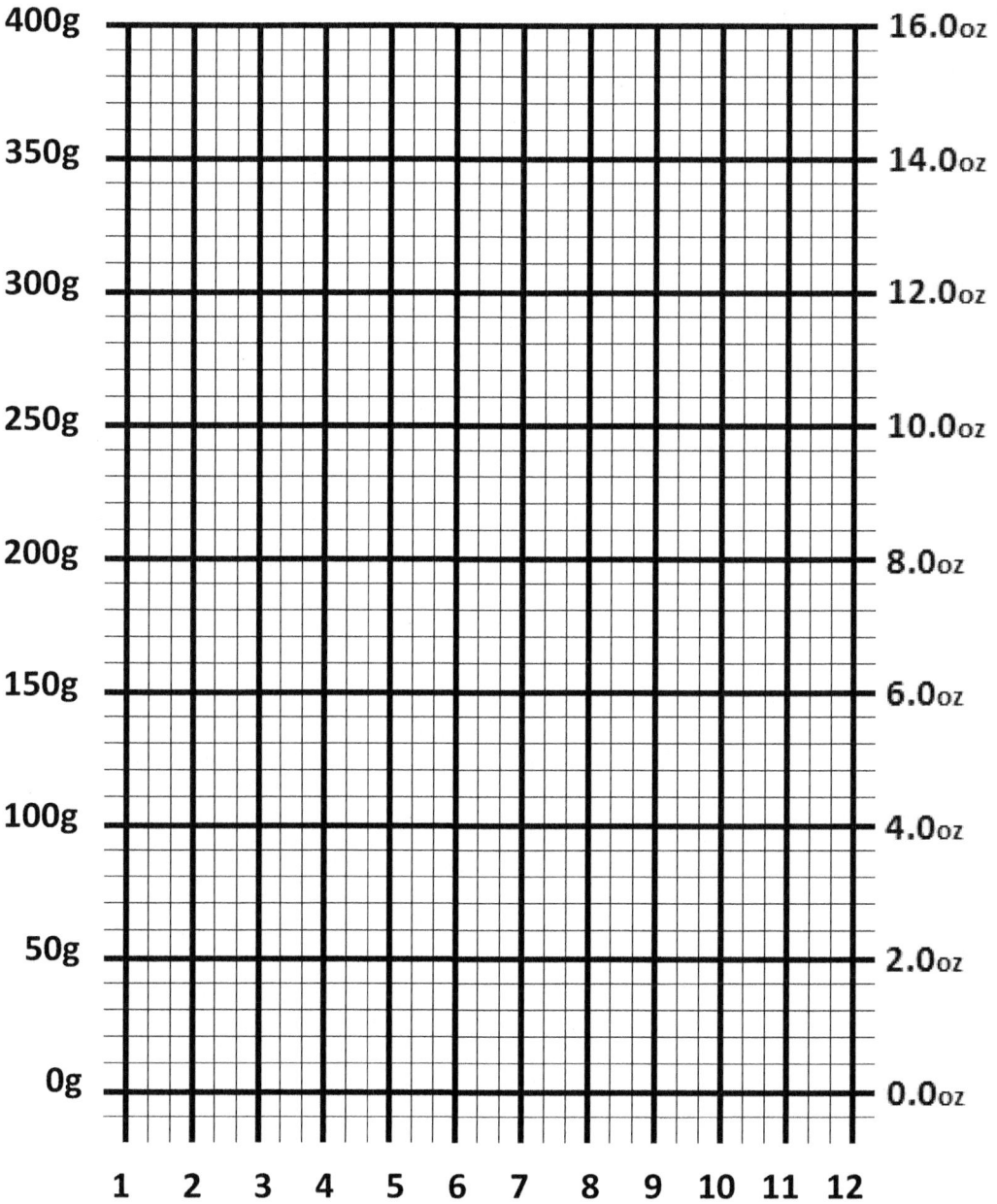

GRAPH

	400g												16.0oz
	350g												14.0oz
	300g												12.0oz
	250g												10.0oz
	200g												8.0oz
	150g												6.0oz
	100g												4.0oz
	50g												2.0oz
	0g												0.0oz

1   2   3   4   5   6   7   8   9   10   11   12

WEIGHT (11)

Date	Weight	Comments

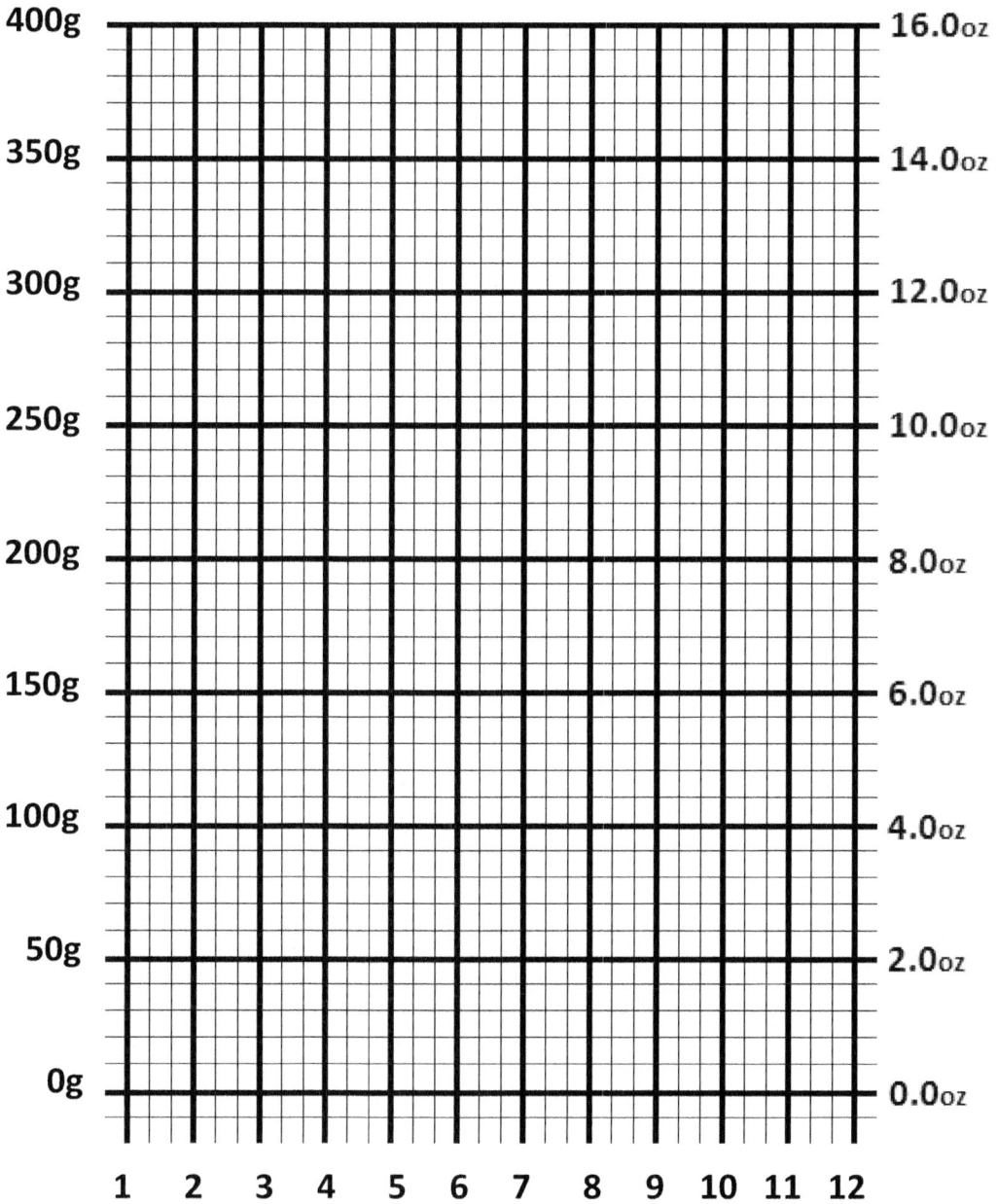

GRAPH

400g — 16.0oz

350g — 14.0oz

300g — 12.0oz

250g — 10.0oz

200g — 8.0oz

150g — 6.0oz

100g — 4.0oz

50g — 2.0oz

0g — 0.0oz

1 2 3 4 5 6 7 8 9 10 11 12

WEIGHT (12)

Date	Weight	Comments

GRAPH

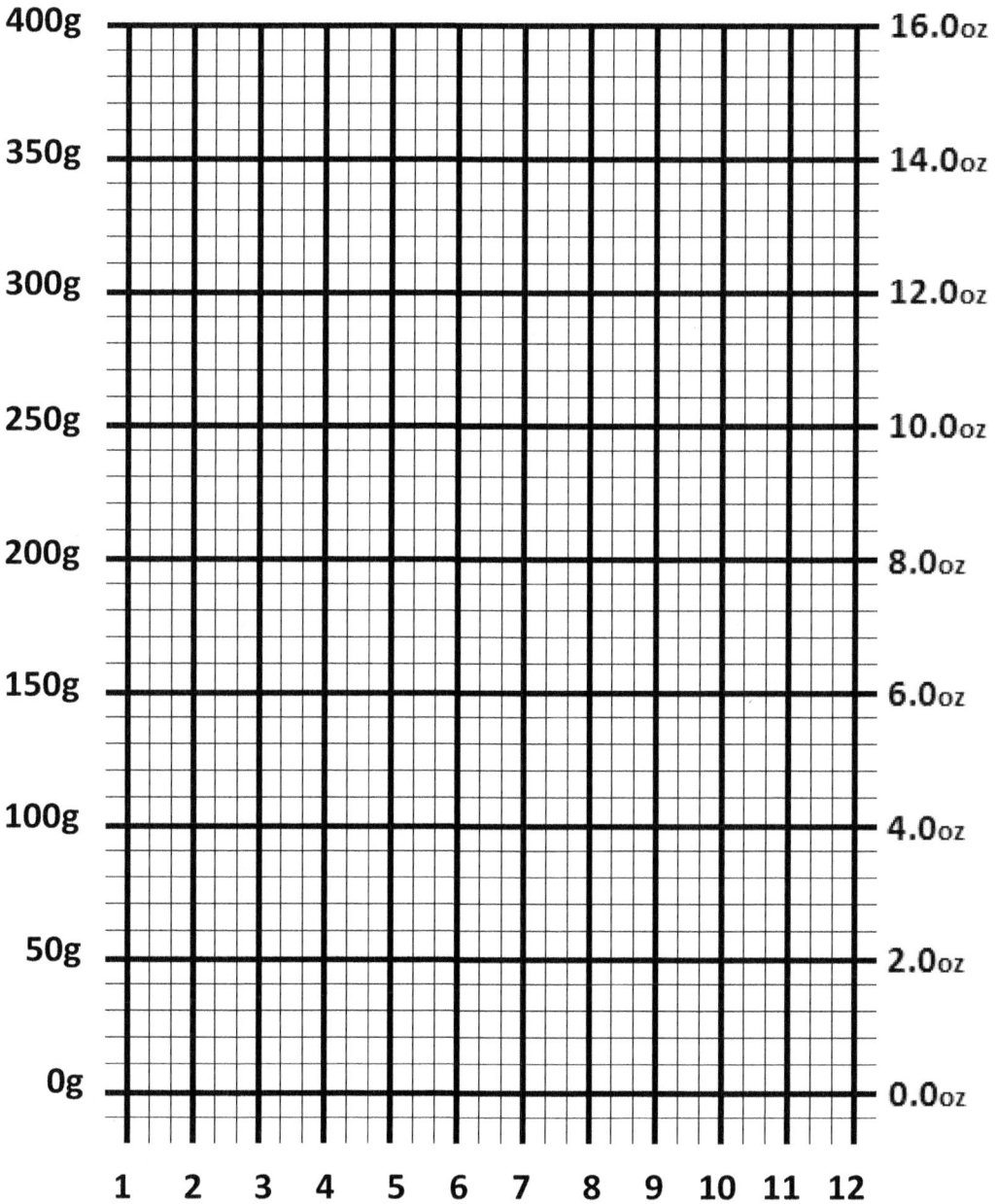

400g												16.0oz
350g												14.0oz
300g												12.0oz
250g												10.0oz
200g												8.0oz
150g												6.0oz
100g												4.0oz
50g												2.0oz
0g	1	2	3	4	5	6	7	8	9	10	11	12	0.0oz

COMMENTS

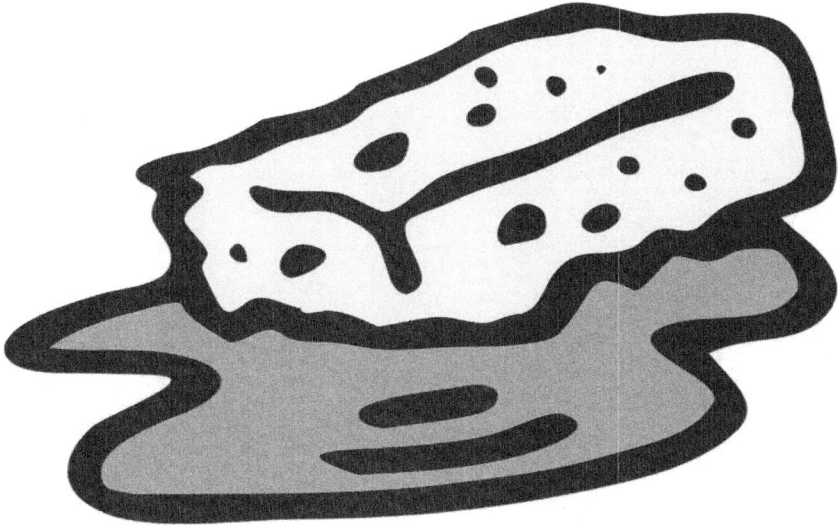

MONTHLY CARE

CARE

Date	Comments

CARE

Date	Comments

CARE

Date	Comments

CARE

Date	Comments

CARE

Date	Comments

CARE

Date	Comments

CARE

Date	Comments

CARE

Date	Comments

CARE

Date	Comments

REPRODUCTION

REPRODUCTION N°1

MATING

Hibernation	Temperatures	Partner 1	Partner 2
from		from	from
to		to	to

Last shed before laying eggs :   /   /

INCUBATION

Egg-laying date	Estimated time	Estimated due date	Hatching dat

EGGS

Layed	Viable	Hatched

COMMENTS :

REPRODUCTION N°2

MATING

Hibernation	Temperatures	Partner 1	Partner 2
from		from	from
to		to	to

Last shed before laying eggs :   /   /

INCUBATION

Egg-laying date	Estimated time	Estimated due date	Hatching date

EGGS

Layed	Viable	Hatched

COMMENTS :

REPRODUCTION N°3

MATING

Hibernation	Temperatures	Partner 1	Partner 2
from		from	from
to		to	to

Last shed before laying eggs : ___ / ___ / ___

INCUBATION

Egg-laying date	Estimated time	Estimated due date	Hatching dat·

EGGS

Layed	Viable	Hatched

COMMENTS :

_____

_____

_____

REPRODUCTION N°4

MATING

Hibernation	Temperatures	Partner 1	Partner 2
from		from	from
to		to	to

Last shed before laying eggs : ___ / ___ / ___

INCUBATION

Egg-laying date	Estimated time	Estimated due date	Hatching date

EGGS

	Layed	Viable	Hatched

COMMENTS :

_____

_____

_____

REPRODUCTION N°5

MATING

Hibernation	Temperatures	Partner 1	Partner 2
from		from	from
to		to	to

Last shed before laying eggs : /   /

INCUBATION

Egg-laying date	Estimated time	Estimated due date	Hatching dat

EGGS

Layed	Viable	Hatched

COMMENTS :

REPRODUCTION N°6

MATING

Hibernation	Temperatures	Partner 1	Partner 2
from		from	from
to		to	to

Last shed before laying eggs :   /   /

INCUBATION

Egg-laying date	Estimated time	Estimated due date	Hatching date

EGGS

Layed	Viable	Hatched

COMMENTS :

REPRODUCTION N°7

MATING

Hibernation	Temperatures	Partner 1	Partner 2
from		from	from
to		to	to

Last shed before laying eggs :   /   /

INCUBATION

Egg-laying date	Estimated time	Estimated due date	Hatching date

EGGS

Layed	Viable	Hatched

COMMENTS :

REPRODUCTION N°8

MATING

Hibernation	Temperatures	Partner 1	Partner 2
from		from	from
to		to	to

Last shed before laying eggs :   /   /

INCUBATION

Egg-laying date	Estimated time	Estimated due date	Hatching date

EGGS

Layed	Viable	Hatched

COMMENTS :

REPRODUCTION N°9

MATING

Hibernation	Temperatures	Partner 1	Partner 2
from		from	from
to		to	to

Last shed before laying eggs :   /   /

INCUBATION

Egg-laying date	Estimated time	Estimated due date	Hatching dat

EGGS

Layed	Viable	Hatched

COMMENTS :

REPRODUCTION N°10

MATING

Hibernation	Temperatures	Partner 1	Partner 2
from		from	from
to		to	to

Last shed before laying eggs :   /   /

INCUBATION

Egg-laying date	Estimated time	Estimated due date	Hatching date

EGGS

Layed	Viable	Hatched

COMMENTS :

REPRODUCTION N°11

MATING

Hibernation	Temperatures	Partner 1	Partner 2
from		from	from
to		to	to

Last shed before laying eggs : /   /

INCUBATION

Egg-laying date	Estimated time	Estimated due date	Hatching dat‹

EGGS

Layed	Viable	Hatched

COMMENTS :

COMMENTS

COMMENTS

COMMENTS

<u>COMMENTS</u>

COMMENTS

COMMENTS

COMMENTS

COMMENTS

COMMENTS

<u>COMMENTS</u>

VETERINARY

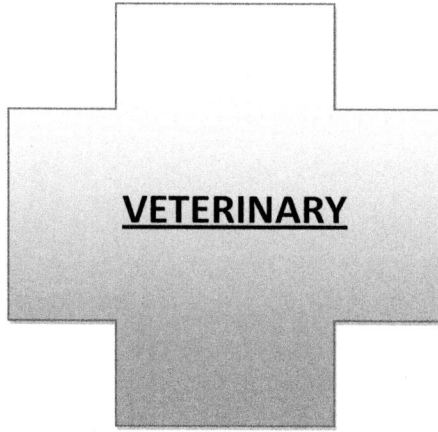

VETERINARY

Date	

133

134

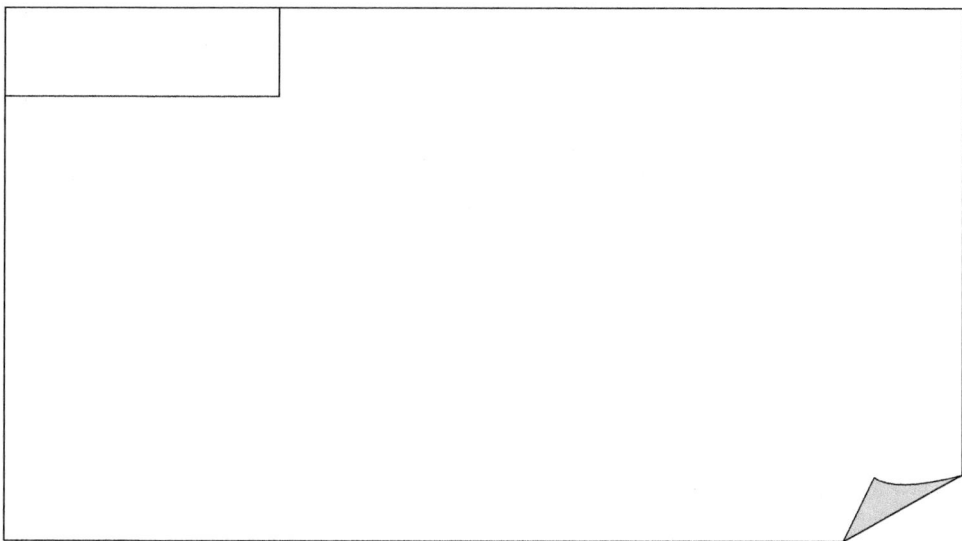

135

136

137

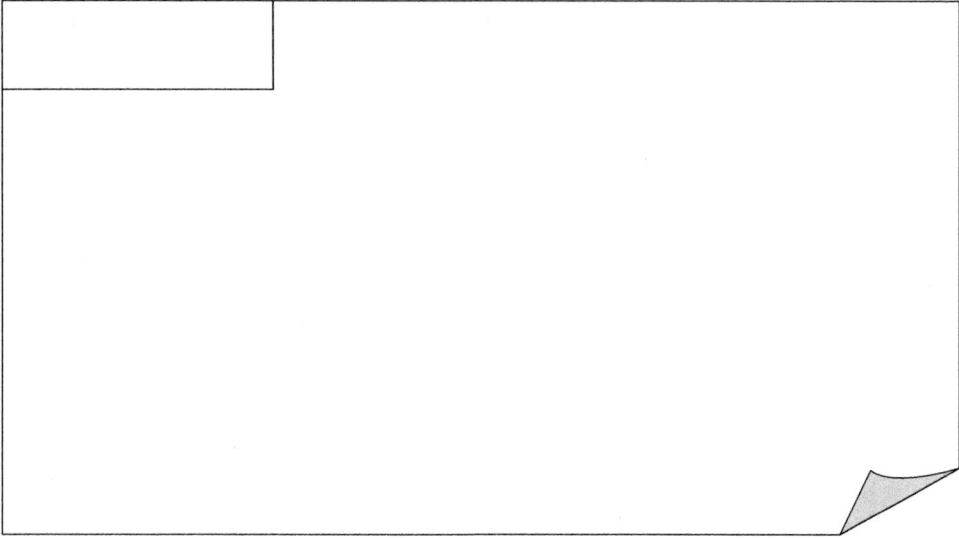

138

---> **Also Available :**

Lizard log books :

- CAMAELEO calyptratus - Yemen Chameleon
- CORRELOPHUS ciliatus - Crested Gecko
- EUBLEPHARIS macularius - Leopard Gecko
- FURCIFER pardalis - Panther Chameleon
- LEPIDOTHYRIS fernandi - Fire Skink
- PHELSUMA grandis – Madagascar Giant Day Gecko
- PHYSIGNATHUS cocincinus – Chinese Water Dragon
- POGONA henrylawsoni - Rankin's dragon
- POGONA vitticeps - Bearded dragon

Simplified log book: (Only line, no text)

- CUBARIS Rubber Ducky
- CUBARIS Jupiter

--- > More log book to come ! ! !

Instagram: benjamin_edeine_editions

Facebook: Benjamin Edeine Editions

Printed in Great Britain
by Amazon